Sanguine-Melancholy
Workbook

The Performer Pattern

How To Develop Your Natural Tendencies and Deal With Your Strengths and Weaknesses Biblically

John T. Cocoris, Th.M., Psy.D.

© Temperament Dynamics, LLC
4848 Lemmon Ave.
STE 152
Dallas, TX 75219

www.fourtemperaments.com
info@fourtemperaments.com
512-553-8104

Library of Congress Card Number:
ISBN 978-1-94-84-74-36-8

Temperament Dynamics, LLC
Dallas, Texas 75219

Cover design and interior design and layout by
John T. Cocoris

Printed in the United States of America

Acknowledgements

I am indebted to my wife, Darrellene, who has shared my vision and my passion for the four temperaments. She has reviewed this manuscript and made suggestions that made it better. I am indebted to my brother, Mike, for his guidance and support. He is my mentor.

I am also grateful for Phillip Moss with whom I have spent countless hours talking about the temperament concept of behavior. He has made suggestions that have contributed to the completion of the workbook series.

John 3:16

For God so loved the world that He gave His only begotten Son,
that whoever believes in Him should not perish
but have everlasting life.

Table of Contents

Preface

Author's Note

Table of Contents

PREFACE

I began my journey in 1977 to understand and develop the temperament model of behavior. Along the way I have been a pastor, a corporate consultant, and a professional therapist. I am grateful for the opportunity to have worked with corporations, churches, and those with whom I had the privilege to counsel and coach.

I have written a number of books and manuals on the subject of temperament. This work includes *insights* that I have observed while working with thousands of people in different settings that are not in my other writings.

Previous books include an explanation of all the temperament blends, one on the creative temperament, one for parents, another identifying the seven steps for learning to apply the temperament concept, another explaining why Christians seek counseling, and even one explaining why girls chase guys after a breakup.

A book on how to develop the natural strengths and deal with the natural weaknesses has been requested many times and is long overdue.

A workbook for each temperament blend is a culmination of my life's work that includes my theological training, my experience as a corporate consultant, and my experience as a professional therapist.

This workbook is written for Christians. It is my heart's desire that as you read and apply the information, and the Biblical applications, that you will grow in the grace and knowledge of Jesus Christ and become more like Him.

John T. Cocoris
McKinney, Texas

Temperament knowledge is to life
what oil is to a machine,
it makes it run smother.

John 13:34-35

A new commandment I give to you, that you love one another:
just as I have loved you, you also are to love one another.
By this all people will know that you are my disciples,
if you have love for one another.

Author's Note

I have written a series of books and manuals on the subject of temperament. Each work represents a different application of the temperament concept. In order to adequately understand each application it is necessary to include in each work a variation of the history of the temperament concept, foundational principles, and common questions. If this is the only book you read on the subject of the temperaments then you would need the information in Part I. The material found in Part I is also found in more detail in my book, *Why We Do What We Do, New Insights Into The Temperament Model of Behavior,* *2020.* This work contains excerpts from other books that I have written.

This workbook is design for someone that has takened the *Four Temperaments Assessment.* You can take the assessment by going to *www.fourtemperaments.com.*

Matthew 18:21-22

Then Peter came up and said to Him, "Lord, how often will my brother sin against me, and I forgive him? As many as seven times?" Jesus said to him, "I do not say to you seven times, but seventy times seven.

PART I

The History & Development of The Four-Temperaments

You are **not** a product of
your environment or
circumstances,

you are a product of
your **choices**.

Chapter 1

Introduction

The concept of the four temperaments does not appear in the Bible. We can, however, see the behavior of the four temperaments in the men and women of the Bible.

Temperament
Each temperament has both strengths and weaknesses. By knowing your temperament blend you will be more aware of your natural strengths and natural weaknesses. There are steps provided that will help you use your natural strengths and overcome the impact of your natural weaknesses on yourself and others.

The Goal is Christ Likeness
The goal of this workbook is to help Christians, using the knowledge of their temperament blend, and Biblical concepts, to grow spiritually and to become more like Christ.

Three Separations
Most people do not understand why they behave the way they do. There is a disconnect within that is perplexing. Many have asked, "Why did I do that?" The answer is a combination of having a sin nature (as a result of Adam's sin) and possessing natural tendencies referred to as temperament. The consequences of Adam's sin is three separations which occurred immediately after he sinned:

1. Separation from God (Genesis 3:1-11).
2. Separation from the woman (Genesis 3:12, 20).
3. Separation from within himself (Romans 7:19-20).

   Jeremiah 17:9 *The heart is deceitful above all things, and desperately wicked; Who can know it?*

   Romans 7:19-20 *For the good that I will to do, I do not do; but the evil I will not to do, that I practice. 20 Now if I do what I will not to do, it is no longer I who do it, but sin that dwells in me.*

As a result we do not understand our internal motivations and drives. Knowing your temperament blend identifies that which is normal and natural which will enable you to first become *aware*, and then *control*, specific thoughts, feelings, and behaviors on your spiritual journey to become more like Jesus Christ.

Be Doers

This workbook will offer Biblical principles for you to put into practice. **James 1:22** says, *But be doers of the word, and not hearers only, deceiving yourselves.*

Johari's Window

The Johari Window, named after the first names of its inventors, Joseph Luft and Harry Ingham, is one of the most useful models explaining our awareness or lack thereof. A four paned "window," as illustrated below, divides personal awareness into four different categories, as represented by its four quadrants: open, blind, hidden, and unknown. The lines dividing the four panes are like window shades which can move as more self-awareness is achieved.

Admittedly, it is a difficult thing to really know yourself (much less someone else). Few people take the time to even try to figure out *why they do what they do*. Most seem content not to know even though they may wonder. Some live their life in the dark never really understanding themselves or being aware of their behavior and how it impacts others.

People have different levels of self-awareness. There is the *open self*, this part of a person is known to yourself and to others. There is the *concealed self*, this part is not known to you, but known to others. There is the *secret self*, this part is known to you, but unknown to others. Then there is the *invisible self*, this part is unknown to you and others. This reveals that there are naturally some things you do not know about yourself. Some things remain a secret, even to you.

Known to Self	Unknown to Self
OPEN	**BLIND**
Known to Others	Known to Others
Known to Self	Unknown to Self
HIDDEN	**UNKNOWN**
Unknown to Others	Unknown to Others

It is helpful, enlightening and encouraging, to discover the natural tendencies with which you were born. This information may open the *window* and allow you to see something about your *concealed* and *invisible* self.

The purpose of this workbook, in part, includes you becoming more *aware* of the expression of your natural temperament tendencies. Being more aware take *ownership* of your natural tendencies to consciously express the controlled strengths and develop a plan to overcome the negative impact of your weaknesses on yourself and others.

Chapter 2

History of The Four Temperaments: Significant Contributors

Throughout history there have been many attempts to explain *why people do what they do*. One of the first systems developed was astrology which looked *outside* of man to explain behavior.

The idea that a person's behavior is the result of being born with natural traits or tendencies (temperament) has been around for at least 2,400 years. However, there is evidence that it's been around much longer than that.

Those listed below are the pioneers that have made the most significant contributions to the development of the temperament model of behavior.

Hippocrates of Kos (C. 460-377 B.C.)

Hippocrates, the father of modern medicine, looked *inside* of man to explain the differences in people's behavior. He taught that behavior (temperament) was determined by the presence, in excess, of one of four *biles* or *humors*:

Yellow Bile | An excess of yellow bile (Chlor) resulted in a temperament (Choleric) believed to be warm/hot and dry and associated with the element of fire.

Red Bile | An excess of red bile (Sangis) resulted in a temperament (Sanguine) believed to be warm/hot and wet and associated with the element of air.

White Bile | An excess of white bile (Phlegm) resulted in a temperament (Phlegmatic) believed to be cool/cold and wet and associated with the element of earth.

Black Bile | An excess of black bile (Melan) resulted in a temperament (Melancholy) believed to be cool/cold and dry and associated with the element of water.

The word temperament comes from the Latin word *temperamentum* and means "right blending." Hippocrates postulated that an imbalance among the four biles/humors resulted in pain and disease and that good health was achieved through a balance of the four biles/humors. For many years this idea was held as the foundation of medicine.

Since the time of Hippocrates the temperament concept was used as the basic explanation for *why people do what they do*. The temperament concept lost popularity when modern psychology began in 1879.

Hippocrates and the early Greeks were accurate in their observations of behavior but were incorrect about the origin of these tendencies. These tendencies are not, of course, created by the presence of a fluid. Today, we would say that they originate from some genetic predisposition although we cannot be certain.

Galen of Pergamon (AD 129-200 or 216)

Galen was a Greek physician who lived 600 years after Hippocrates and was responsible for popularizing the temperaments during his time and relating them to illness. He is also credited with coining the terms Choleric (from Chlor), Sanguine (from Sangis), Phlegmatic (from Phlegm), and Melancholy (from Melan).

Nicholas Culpeper (1616-1654)

He was the first to dispute two fundamental concepts that had existed since the time of Hippocrates. First, he rejected the idea that the four "humors" were the cause of a person's temperament. Secondly, he was the first to say that a person is influenced by two temperaments, one primary and one secondary. Before Culpeper, it was believed that a person had only one temperament.

Immual Kant (1724-1804)

He described the four temperaments in his book, *Anthropology from a Pragmatic Point of View*, 1798. These excerpts are from his book and shows the consistency and enduring nature of human behavior:

The Choleric Temperament of The Hot-Blooded Man. We say of a choleric man that he is fiery, burns up quickly like straw-fire, and can be readily appeased if others give in to him; there is no hatred in his anger, and in fact he loves someone all the more for promptly giving in to him.

The Sanguine Temperament of The Volatile Man. A sanguine person is carefree and attaches great importance to each thing for the moment, and the next moment may not give it another thought. He is a good companion, high-spirited, and all men are his friends.

The Phlegmatic Temperament of The Cold-Blooded Man. Phlegma means apathy, dullness; phlegma as weakness is a tendency to inactivity, not to let oneself be moved even by strong incentives for getting busy. He is not easily angered, but reflects first whether he should get angry.

The Melancholy Temperament of The Grave Man. A man disposed to melancholy attaches great importance to everything that has to do with himself. He finds grounds for apprehension everywhere and directs his attention first to the difficulties. The melancholy temperament thinks deeply.

Kant taught that a society should be based on appreciating the temperament differences in people.

William Moulton Marston (1894-1949)

Dr. Marston was the first to contribute scientific evidence that people fit into one of four categories. He studied the emotions of normal people and through his research identified four distinctively different behavioral responses to specific environments and people. He then selected 35 words or phrases that represented the four different approaches.

Marston's research determined that when a person is faced with a *favorable* or *unfavorable* situation two things happen. First, there is a neurological event caused by the perception of the stimuli in the environment (favorable or unfavorable). Second, a message is sent to the motor self (that which causes movement) to either move toward the stimuli, to move away from the stimuli, or not move at all.

He published his book *Emotions of Normal People* in 1928 using the terms Dominance, Inducement, Submission, and Compliance. Here are the four categories and the summary of his research:

Dominance [Choleric] This person has active, positive movement in an unfavorable (antagonistic) environment to overcome the opposition to get their desired results.

Inducement [Sanguine] This person has active, positive movement in a favorable or friendly environment to enjoy socializing.

Submission [Phlegmatic] This person is passive in both a favorable and unfavorable environment.

Compliance [Melancholy] This person has two responses in an unfavorable (antagonistic) environment. The *first* response is to withdraw. After the situation has been analyzed and a plan developed, the *second* response is to be assertive to bring resolve. In a favorable environment they will move forward to enforce the rules and offer organization.

Here are a few little known facts about Dr. Marston: he was also responsible for the invention of the *systolic blood-pressure test* which he attached to the current version of the *lie detector*. He also created the cartoon character, *Wonder Woman*.

Ole Hallesby (1879-1961)

Ole Hallesby, a Lutheran theology professor in Norway, contributed penetrating insight into the behavior of the four temperaments. He wrote *Temperament And The Christian Faith*, 1940; he used the terms Choleric, Sanguine, Phlegmatic, and Melancholy.

The book by Hallesby is limited in that he discusses behavior as it relates to the four *primary* temperaments and did not write about the dynamics of the combinations. However, his insights into the behavior of the temperaments are unsurpassed in the writings that I have reviewed. For the serious student of the four temperaments this book is a must read.

Hans J. Eysenck (1916-1997)

Dr. Eysenck in *Personality and Individual Differences, A Natural Science Approach,* 1985, (p. 3), sums up the concept of temperament this way:

> This was pioneered by Hippocrates and later canonized by Galen, a Roman physician who lived in the second century A.D. It is to these men and to the many others who worked in this field that we owe the doctrine of the four temperaments: phlegmatic, sanguine, choleric, and melancholic. The highly successful typology thus established all those years ago was based on careful observation and provided a paradigm for scientific investigation that has lasted over 2,000 years and may still have something to teach us.

Dr. Eysenck has written other books on the subject including, *The Biological Basis of Personality* (1967).

Tim LaHaye (1926-2016)

Tim LaHaye was the first to popularize the temperament concept within the Christian community. Dr. LaHaye published the first of several books in the 1960's using the terms Choleric, Sanguine, Phlegmatic, and Melancholy. He was the first to write in detail about the dynamics of the temperament blends.

John G. Geier (1934-2009)

John G. Geier built on the previous works of William M. Marston (1928), Walter Clarke (1940), and John Cleaver (1950). Walter Clarke developed the *Activity Vector Analysis* using the four dimensions of Aggressive, Sociable, Stable, and Avoidant.

Building on Clarke's work, John Cleaver created the first 24-question, forced-choice instrument. Building on the works of these men, John Geier developed the *Personal Profile* instrument in 1972 (later called the *Personal Profile System,* 1977) that identified an individual's behavioral style. John Geier coined the terms High D (Dominance), High I (Inducement), High S (Submission), and High C (Compliance). He created the acronym DiSC.

John Cocoris (1943-Today)

Dr. Cocoris built on the works of those who have been mentioned plus his own research. He developed the DISCII, DISC3, *discstrengths,* and *fourtemperaments* assessments. He pioneered the development of a system to verbally validate a person's temperament blend. His research and writings were based on personally interviewing thousands of people all across the USA. He has published numerous books and manuals on the subject of temperament and is the author of this work.

Others

Others have contributed to the concept of *temperament* including Plato (350 BC), Paracelsus (1530), Adickes (1905), Spranger (1914), Kretschmer (1930), Adler (1937), Fromm (1947), Eysenck (1951), and Keirsey (1970).

TEMPERAMENT MODEL DEVIATIONS

The researchers mentioned above have maintained the original concept that there are four categories of behavior. They have expanded our knowledge with their observations and insights. There have been others, however, who have deviated from the historical flow by adding concepts that have caused confusion rather than clarity. Included in these, in my opinion, are Carl Jung and Isabel Myers. Both have been criticized for their lack of clarity and apparent contradictions.

The original observations made over thousands of years have been proven to be consistent and accurate. Any system that deviates from it is incomplete, sometimes incorrect, and even misleading. Virtually all current approaches represent fragments of the four temperaments without a reference to the history from which it is based.

Carl Jung (1875-1961)

Carl Jung, a Swiss psychiatrist, published *Psychological Types* in 1921. He was searching for answers as to why people were different. The premise of his work was to determine how people take in information and make decisions.

Jung coined the terms *extrovert* and *introvert* (1921) suggesting that everyone falls into one of the two categories. The extrovert prefers the outer, objective world of things, people, and actions. Whereas the introvert prefers the inner, subjective world of thoughts, ideas, and emotions.

Jung identified four mental functions that he combined with *extroversion* and *introversion*: thinking (logical, objective); feeling (subjective experience); sensation (stimuli from the senses); and intuitive (creative, imaginative and integrative). Jung's system has eight basic personality types: extroverted thinker, extroverted feeler, extroverted sensor, extroverted intuitor, introverted thinker, introverted feeler, introverted sensor, and introverted intuitor.

There is some correlation between Jung's system and the original four temperaments by Hippocrates but at best it is not clear. However, Jung made a valuable contribution by giving us the concepts of *extrovert* and *introvert*.

Isable Myers (1897-1980), Katherine Briggs (1875-1968)

Isabel Briggs Myers and her mother-in-law, Katherine Cook-Briggs, wrote a paper in 1958 titled, "Myers-Briggs Type Indicator (MBTI)" in which they proposed that there are sixteen different personality types. Their work was based on Carl Jung's writings on psychological types. In their system, a person has two choices for orientation; introvert (I) or extrovert (E); two choices for method of information intake sensing (S) or intuition (N); two choices for method of judgment, thinking (T) or feeling (F); and two choices to use in the outer world of judgment (J) or perception (P). These combine to make up 16 personality types.

The Myers-Briggs Type Indicator is a popular and widely used instrument but it is not without controversy. David J. Pittenger, Ph.D., made the following comments in his evaluation of the MBTI:

> There are several reports of the test retest reliabilities of the four dimensions of the MBTI (Carskadon, 1977, 1979; Howes & Carskadon, 1979; Stricker & Ross, 1962). These

reports offer a consistent pattern that suggests that the reliability of the MBTI does not meet expectations derived from its theory" (Cautionary Comments Regarding the Myers-Briggs Type Indicator, published in 2005 in Consulting Psychology Journal: Practice and Research, Vol. 57, No. 3, 214).

The Myers Brigg Type Indicator does not allow for a person to be a combination of an *Extroverted* (E) and *Introverted* (I) combination. This is a major error of the MBTI assessment.

The temperament model of behavior demonstrates that a person can be an extrovert/introvert or introvert/extrovert combination; for example, the Sanguine-Melancholy is an extrovert/introvert combination and the Melancholy-Sanguine is an introvert/extrovert combination.

Summary. The ancient Greeks observed people and speculated on the reasons for their behavior. Their observations were supported in later centuries by a wide variety of people including medical doctors and philosophers.

In the early 1900's, the scientific method was applied by Marston with the same results. The concept that people fall into four categories has been observed for over two thousand years, verified by the scientific method, and everyone describes them basically the same. The four temperament model illustrates the consistency and enduring nature of human behavior.

Chapter 3

Frequently Asked Questions

1. WHAT IS TEMPERAMENT?

Temperament is Not The Same As Character

Temperament has nothing to do with a person's character or their level of maturity. It is what a person is naturally. Here is my definition:

**Temperament is a cluster of inborn
traits that causes you, in part,
to do what you do.**

Temperament is Not a "Type"

A distinction needs to be made between a "trait" and a "type." "Types" are considered to be categories into which a person may either *fit* or *not fit*. For example, a person could be seen as either an *extrovert* or *introvert*.

Temperament Represents a Cluster of "Traits"

Temperament is a cluster of inborn traits that causes you, in part, to do what you do, naturally. Temperament, therefore, represents the core foundational tendencies or drives that make up an individual.

The four temperaments are represented by four distinct groups of traits or tendencies. Each cluster of traits produces a distinct manner of behavior that is different from the other three groups. For example, the Choleric is result-oriented, the Sanguine is people-oriented, the Phlegmatic is service-oriented, and the Melancholy is quality-oriented.

Each trait can be placed on a continuum from low expression to high expression. For example, one may possess the trait of being social to a high degree, moderate degree, or almost not at all. A trait is like a rheostat switch that controls a light. When you turn the switch up the light gets *brighter,* when you turn the switch down the lights gets *dimmer*. The more of a given trait one possess, the more observable it will be in their behavior.

The temperament model embraces the trait approach which allows for a particular trait to be possessed and developed to varying degrees. Temperament represents natural traits or tendencies with which a person is born. How well these natural traits are developed depends on the individual's choices.

Arnold Buss and Robert Plomin (1975) give Gordon Allport's definition of temperament in *A Temperament Theory of Personality Development*:

Temperament refers to the characteristic phenomena of an individual's nature, including his susceptibility to emotional stimulation, his customary strength and speed of response, the quality of his prevailing mood, and all the peculiarities of fluctuation and intensity of mood, these being phenomena regarded as dependent on constitutional makeup, and therefore largely hereditary in origin.

John Geier (1983), in *The Library of Classical Patterns*, describes temperament this way:

During a lifetime we experience many emotions, but there is an emotional state which is most characteristic for each of us. We depart from that basic temperament when aroused by such feelings as love, hate, sadness, anger, rage, or exuberance. However, these emotions tend to be as transient as they are intense. Love slips through our fingers; hate is difficult to sustain for long periods; joy and sorrow eventually dissipate. Like strong winds, these emotions temporarily ruffle the surface of our usual emotional demeanor. When others describe us with such words as friendly, logical, aggressive, or careful, they are referring to the feeling state we usually project. That state reflects our self-concept and has evolved from genetic predispositions and the shaping forces of the environment. Others may approve or disapprove of our temperament. It may meld or conflict with the expectations of groups or organizations. The crucial aspect is recognizing the "given" of our emotions and choosing the environment in which we will be accepted and productive.

Temperament Behavior is What a Person is *Most* of The Time

Temperament behavior represents the way a person relates to others and responds to events. It is what you have observed and expect someone's behavior to be.

Have you ever referred to someone as shy or outgoing? Without realizing it you were referring to certain temperament traits. These traits are what you know and expect the person to be every time you are with them. Thus, temperament behavior is, for the most part, predictable. The exception being when one temporarily experiences strong emotions, such as anger or fear, or is trying to deceive another. Actually, acting is a form of acceptable deception. A person is knowingly acting like they are someone else. Unfortunately, some purposely act like someone they are not in order to deceive.

Society would not be able to exist if behavior were not predictable. Imagine what life would be like if everyone were different every time you met them. Imagine the chaos. Without consistency in people, without predictability, any society simply would not survive.

Temperament is a *Drive*

Temperament is a *drive* or *force* within that represents various traits or tendencies that produce an *urge* that creates an *appetite*. Temperament urges and even drives a person to act in a particular manner. Temperament, as an appetite or void, requires satisfaction. An obvious illustration is when you are hungry you have a need to eat; it's a void to be satisfied. When you eat, the void is filled and you are satisfied and no longer hungry. Temperament is that way. It pushes or urges you to behave according to the tendencies that represent your temperament combination.

For example, there are those who are naturally *people-oriented*. They enjoy being with, around, or just standing by others. They like to talk, have fun, and be active with others. There is a drive/force within these people that urges them to do this. Ask those with the Sanguine temperament and they will tell you "I just like being with people." Conversely, there are those who are private in nature and they prefer *not* to be with, around, or by others. There is an equal force within them that urges or drives them to avoid contact with others. Both are normal drives that urge a person to meet their natural yet different needs.

Temperament is a *Need*

Abraham Maslow says that a *need* is something that if not met will make you sick. Air, food, and water, are physical needs without which a person would become physically ill and die. Temperament represents needs but no one will die without those needs being met. A temperament *need* represents what is important and highly desirable in the core of an individual.

Temperament is a *need* that urges, drives and motivates a person to act according to their natural tendencies. If temperament *needs* are not met, the individual will not feel at peace or function efficiently. Meeting temperament *needs* is, therefore, critical to a person's sense of well-being and feeling of self-worth.

Let's again use the Sanguine temperament as an example. As a *people-person* the Sanguine enjoys social involvement. This includes talking to others or just being in the presence of one or more people. Social contact is a *need* of the Sanguine temperament and if not met the person will not feel okay about themselves. This is just one of the four temperaments. The others will have specific *needs* as does this one but all will be different from each other. The Choleric, for example, *needs* to see results quickly; the Phlegmatic *needs* to follow a routine; the Melancholy *needs* to have a detailed plan. These *needs* are both normal and natural. Everyone, therefore, should provide adequate satisfaction for their temperament *needs* in order to be at their best.

2. FROM WHERE DID WE GET OUR TEMPERAMENT?

There are two possibilities. Either people are born *without* natural tendencies or they are born *with* natural tendencies.

People Are Born *Without* Natural Tendencies

Some believe that people start life as a blank slate (tabula rasa) and that the environment determines their personality. Dr. James Dobson (1987) is not in favor of this position but reports it in *Parenting Isn't for Cowards*:

> Sigmund Freud, the father of Psychoanalysis, and J.B. Watson, the creator of behaviorism, believed that newborns come into the world as "blank slates" on which the environment would later write. For them a baby had no inborn characteristics of personality that

distinguished him from other infants. Everything he would become, both good and evil, would result from the experiences to be provided by the world around him. He could make no independent decisions because he had no real freedom of choice ... no ability to consider his circumstances and to act rationally on them. Watson even rejected the existence of a mind.

The view that tendencies are acquired was also stated by David Merrill and Roger Reid (1981) in *Personal Styles & Effective Performance*:

Why do people develop these behavioral preferences? ... people tend to do things that make them feel comfortable. Once a pattern of actions receives positive reinforcement, we have a tendency to repeat it.

People Are Born *With* Natural Tendencies

This position teaches that a person is born with natural tendencies and that they are developed according to the person's response to their environment. In the article "Born to be Shy?" Jules Asher (1987) wrote the following concerning Dr. Jerome Kagan's research:

We've all met shy toddlers — the ones who cling to their parents and only reluctantly venture into an unfamiliar room. Faced with strangers, they first freeze, falling silent and staring at them. They seem visibly tense until they've had a chance to size up the new scene. Parents of such children are likely to say they've always been on the timid side. 'It's just his way,' one might say.

Arnold Buss and Robert Plomin (1975) discuss this position in their book, *A Temperament Theory of Personality Development*:

To aid understanding, we shall start with a non temperament model of personality. This model assumes that each person starts as a blank slate (tabula rasa) that will be written on by experience. It assumes that man's nature is that he has no nature. It flatly rejects the possibility of inborn tendencies that determine individual differences in personality. Environment is all. If there are stable individual differences, they are learned during childhood, during adulthood, or both. We have no quarrel with this model if it is restricted to some aspects of personality. There is presently no basis for assuming that differences among persons in self-esteem, guilt, or authoritarianism are derived from inborn dispositions. These and many other aspects of personality would seem to be wholly acquired during the course of living. But we cannot accept this model for all aspects of personality. Some behavioral tendencies - we would argue, some of the most basic personality tendencies - originate in inherited dispositions.

Dr. James Dobson (1987) discusses temperaments in his book, *Parenting Isn't for Cowards*:

> It is my supposition that these temperaments are prepackaged before birth and do not have to be cultivated or encouraged. They will make themselves known soon enough. Behavioral scientists are now observing and documenting the subtle understandings that have been evident in Scriptures for thousands of years. One of the most ambitious of these efforts to study temperaments of babies has been in progress for more than three decades. It is known as the New York Longitudinal Study, 1969. The findings from this investigation, led by psychiatrists Stella Chess and Alexander Thomas, are now reported in their excellent book for parents entitled, *Know Your Child.* To my delight, Chess and Thomas found that babies not only differ significantly from one another at the moment of birth, but those differences tend to be rather persistent throughout childhood.

In their book *Personality Structure & Measurement*, Dr. Hans Eysenck and Sybil Eysenck (1969) state that traits are rooted in genetics:

> These early ideas developed by Greek writers, thinkers and physicians already contain, if only in embryo, the three main notions which characterize modern work in personality. In the first place, behavior or conduct is to be described in terms of traits which characterize given individuals in varying degrees. In the second place, these traits cohere or correlate and define certain more fundamental and more all-embracing types. In the third place, these types are essentially based on constitutional, genetic or inborn factors, which are to be discovered in the physiological, neurological and biochemical structure of the individual.

Dr. Tim LaHaye (1977), in *Understanding the Male Temperament*, says, "The combination of inherited traits he receives from his parents at the time of conception will determine his eventual temperament."

Finally, perhaps the best proof of all is to ask a mother who has raised at least two children. She will likely tell you that they were different from birth. My daughter has twin girls and knew before they were born that one was going to be active and the other one was going to be laid-back, and that is exactly how they are today.

3. WILL MY TEMPERAMENT BLEND EVER CHANGE?

No. The temperament blend you were born with remains throughout your life. Some are confused about this because they think that because they have experienced some growth that their temperament blend somehow has changed. When in fact all that has happened is they have learned self-control and have matured. There are three areas to consider:

Temporary Modification

There are times when your behavior does not represent your temperament blend but this will always be temporary. A situation may require that you behave in a way that is not natural for you to act, but when the need has passed you will once again behave in a way that represents your temperament blend.

Growth

On occasion, some report that their temperament has changed over the years (e.g., once "shy" and now "outgoing"). I have found this to always be a person with a combination of an extroverted and introverted temperament (e.g., Choleric-Phlegmatic, Sanguine-Melancholy, etc.). There is a way of behaving which you feel is right, good and normal. This represents your "temperament comfort zone" of behavior. When a person suggests that their temperament has changed, they usually mean they had been driven out of their "temperamental comfort zone" by forces in their environment and did not develop their natural tendencies. During their developing years their behavior was represented more by their secondary temperament than their primary one.

We are all influenced by many variables, such as the quality of early home life, education, travel, etc. Regardless of these early influences, as a person develops, they begin to feel more "comfortable" with the way they want to be and are willing to actually behave in that manner. It is not that their temperament has changed, it is simply that they are now expressing the behavior they have always wanted to, they are in their "temperamental comfort zone."

Permanent Modification

It is possible for anyone to control their natural tendencies so that their behavior is modified and does not reflect a particular weakness. For example, the Sanguine has a tendency to talk a lot. Until they learn to moderate the need to verbalize, it can be annoying to others. Once they become aware of this weakness, they can choose to not talk as much thus gaining control over this weakness.

4. ARE TEMPERAMENT AND PERSONALITY THE SAME?

No. They are many factors that make up the total personality of a person. Temperament is only one of the many parts. Stella Chess and Alexander Thomas comment in their book, *Know Your Child*:

> But this recognition of the importance of temperament should not lead to an attempt to equate temperament with personality. We consider personality to be a composite of the enduring psychological attributes that constitute the unique individuality of a person. Personality structure is formed from the many diverse elements that shape psychological development, all acting together: motivations, abilities, interest, temperament, goals and value systems, psychological defense mechanisms, and the impact of the family and the larger sociocultural environment. Temperament is one of the important factors that helps to shape personality, and its influence varies from person to person. Because temperamental

categories or patterns evidence themselves as responses to environmental events and attitudes, the final results of such interactions vary from one person to another. In some instances, one temperamental attribute or pattern may be important in personality development, in other cases a different temperamental attribute may be significant, in still other cases the important temperament pattern may be different again.

5. CAN ANYONE BE A LEADER OR MANAGER REGARDLESS OF THEIR TEMPERAMENT?

Yes. Each person will lead differently according to their temperament blend. The Choleric and Sanguine will lead by *inspiration* (they will *tell* you how to do it). The Phlegmatic and Melancholy will lead by *example* (they will *show* you how to do it). Each one will be effective in their own way. Consider the following Presidents of the United States: Choleric, Lyndon Johnson; Sanguine, Ronald Reagan; Phlegmatic, Gerald Ford; Melancholy, George W. Bush.

6. ARE THE FOUR TEMPERAMENTS IN THE BIBLE?

The Bible does not specifically address people according to this concept nor does the word *temperament* appear in Scripture. The four temperaments are, however, represented in Biblical characters: the Apostle Paul, Choleric; the Apostle Peter, Sanguine; Abraham, Phlegmatic; the Apostle John ,Melancholy.

7. HOW DO THE DIFFERENT NAMES CORRELATE?

There have been many different terms used to refer to the four temperaments. Below is a correlation of some the more popular ones: My personal preference is to use the most archaic terms when referring to the four temperaments; Choleric, Sanguine, Phlegmatic and Melancholy. A descriptive term alone is too narrow, restrictive and limits one's understanding of that particular temperament. A descriptive term will only *suggests* what the person may do in certain situations, it does not represent the essence of the temperament.

For example, a common term used to refer to the Choleric is "Dominant." The Choleric can be dominant but they are not dominant all the time. The term limits our understanding of the Choleric temperament. A common term used to refer to the Sanguine is "Expressive." Indeed they can be expressive but they will not be this all the time. The term limits our understanding of the Sanguine temperament. A common term used to refer to the Phlegmatic is "Amiable." It is true that they can be "amiable" but it is also true that they can stubbornly resist being cooperative. The term limits our understanding of the Phlegmatic temperament. A common term used to refer to the Melancholy is "Compliance", suggesting that they will always be this way. It is true that they can be "compliant" but it is only true if they respect the authority. The term limits our understanding of the Melancholy temperament. A more general term, however, allows for a broad expansion of understanding of a particular temperament. The use of the terms Choleric, Sanguine, Phlegmatic and Melancholy does not bring a narrow bias to the temperaments and leaves open a broad understanding. The point is that a term should not limit understanding or "tag" a temperament with a narrow description.

Correlation of terms.

There have been many different terms used to refer to the four temperaments. Here is a correlation of some the more popular ones:

Choleric	Sanguine	Phlegmatic	Melancholy
High "D"	High "I"	High "S"	High "C"
Dominant	Influencing	Steadiness	Compliance
Directive	Interactive	Supportive	Corrective
Driver	Expressive	Amiable	Analytical
Director	Socializer	Relater	Thinker
Red	Yellow	Gray	Blue

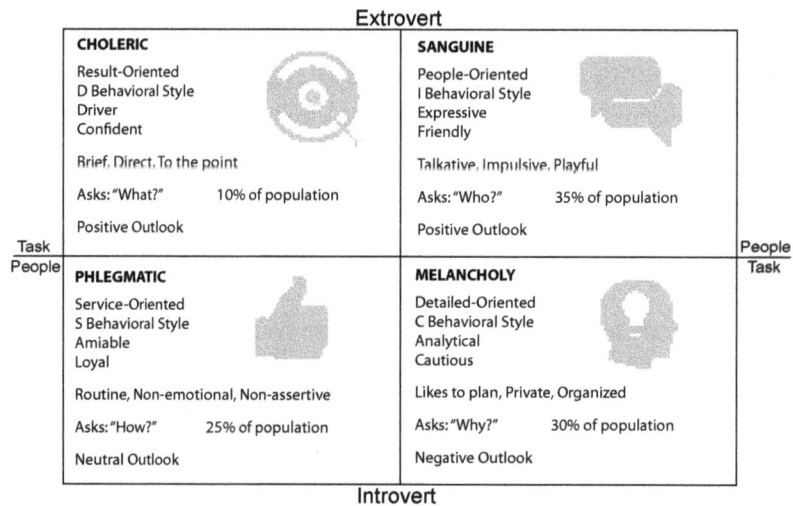

Extrovert

CHOLERIC	SANGUINE
Result-Oriented D Behavioral Style Driver Confident	People-Oriented I Behavioral Style Expressive Friendly
Brief, Direct, To the point	Talkative, Impulsive, Playful
Asks: "What?" 10% of population	Asks: "Who?" 35% of population
Positive Outlook	Positive Outlook
PHLEGMATIC	**MELANCHOLY**
Service-Oriented S Behavioral Style Amiable Loyal	Detailed-Oriented C Behavioral Style Analytical Cautious
Routine, Non-emotional, Non-assertive	Likes to plan, Private, Organized
Asks: "How?" 25% of population	Asks: "Why?" 30% of population
Neutral Outlook	Negative Outlook

Task / People (left side), People / Task (right side)

Introvert

Summary. The ancient Greeks merely made observations about human behavior and speculated on its causes. Their observations were supported in later centuries by physicians and philosophers. In the early 1900's the scientific method was applied by Marston, with the same results. The concept has been observed for centuries and verified by science, that people fall into four categories, and everyone describes the four the same.

PART II

THE
PERFORMER

Sanguine-Melancholy

The better you feel about yourself

the better the world looks!

Chapter 4

The Sanguine-Temperament

The Sanguine temperament has three combinations: Sanguine-Choleric, Sanguine-Phlegmatic, and Sanguine-Melancholy. The traits of the *primary* temperament, Sanguine, will be altered or modified in some significant way due to the influence of the *secondary* temperament.

The Sanguine is naturally people-oriented. The other three temperaments need a reason to be with others socially. Sanguines have an active, positive movement in a favorable environment. They influence their environment by encouraging others to work together.

The Sanguine is by far the most *versatile* of the four temperaments. The Sanguine has the potential for the widest range of behavior due to possessing the widest range of emotions. This allows them to participate (based on their second temperament) in any kind of human activity. They like to participate in, or change, their environment. The areas of business, politics, sports, and entertainment, to name a few, are dominated by the Sanguine temperament.

The Sanguine is extroverted, fun-loving, playful, activity-prone, impulsive, entertaining, persuasive, easily amused, and optimistic. They are enthusiastic, expressive, and tend to be very affectionate. The Sanguine is personable, receptive, open to others, and build relationships quickly. They are animated, excitable, approachable, accepting, and trusting of others. They will smile and talk easily and often; they are a *wordsmith*.

It is not unusual to feel as if you have known one who is Sanguine for years after the first meeting. They make and keep friends easily. They get so involved in conversations that they easily forget about time so they are often late arriving at their destination. The Sanguine is easily bored if not involved in social activity. The Sanguine dislikes solitude. Their attention span is based on whether or not they are interested in the person or event.

When telling a story, the Sanguine may exaggerate what happened or leave out important details. They make the story exciting and they may not let the facts get in the way!

The Sanguine is very competitive. They usually like sports of any kind because of their natural desire to be active and involved with people. They tend to be disorganized and easily forget where they left something. They sometimes have difficulty controlling their thoughts and emotions. Actually, they tend not to store their thoughts and feelings — if they think it or feel it, they share it!

Their voice will show excitement and friendliness. The Sanguine enjoys dressing according to current fashion. They fear rejection or not making a favorable impression. The Sanguine also fears others viewing them as unsuccessful. The Sanguine is very effective working with others.

Note: The above description is not true for all with the Sanguine blends. The basic nature of one who is Sanguine is that they desire to be with others *socially* most of the time. Not all will demonstrate the same high level of excitement and expression as mentioned above.

The philosopher, Immanuel Kant, in his book, *Anthropology from a Pragmatic Point of View* (1798), says this about the Sanguine:

> A sanguine person manifests his way of sensing and can be recognized by the following traits: he is carefree and full of hope; he attaches great importance to each thing for the moment, and the next moment may not give it another thought. He makes promises in all honesty, but fails to keep his word because he has not reflected deeply enough beforehand whether he will be able to keep it. He is a good companion and high-spirited, who is reluctant to take anything seriously and all men are his friends.

The theologian Ole Hallesby in, *Temperament & The Christian Faith*, says this about the Sanguine:

> The sanguine attitude toward one's surroundings is a receptive mood. Impressions from without have easy access to mind and heart. The explanation for this receptivity of spirit lies in the fact that in the sanguine temperament, the feelings are predominant. And it is one's feelings that are most easily stirred by impressions from without.

The following represents behavior of the Sanguine in general. Individual differences will occur based on the influence of the second temperament. Also, what a person is exposed to from an early age plays a vital role in these areas but remember an individual is still responsible for the choices they make. Regardless of one's natural tendencies, discipline applied in any area will control and overcome a weakness, or extreme behavior. The goal is to become a well-balanced person, being in control of thoughts, feelings, and behavior.

Relationships

The Sanguine builds lasting relationships. They make friends easily and often, and enjoy being around people and having fun. They know the largest number of people and will usually have a wide network of friends both personal and professional which is why *Facebook* is so popular! The Sanguine is the affectionate, warm, cozy, "sit by the fire" type.

Time Management

The Sanguine often (but not always) will have difficulty managing their time. When the Sanguine says they will be somewhere at a certain time, they may not mean exactly at that time but somewhere around that time (give or take an hour). They do mean well but they forget about a promise or commitment if they are having a good time where they are!

Money Management

The Sanguine views money as giving them the freedom to enjoy life. Their natural tendency is to spend often on play things, status things, the latest thing, or something they just want. The Sanguine usually wants instant gratification. They see it, they want it, and they feel good when they buy it — not having the money is never a deterrent as long as they have room on one of their many credit cards! One young Sanguine who overdrew on their checking account said "I thought I had money because I still had checks!" Credit card companies and debt counselors love the Sanguine!

Decision Making

The Sanguine frequently makes impulsive decisions. Not much thought may precede a quick decision and consequences are considered later. They often take the approach of "ready ... fire ... aim!"

The Sanguine often expresses remorse for a poor decision but may soon forget the unwanted consequences and repeat the behavior. The Sanguine may have difficulty making an objective decision because they are too concerned about how their decision will make them look in front of others.

Leadership Style

The Sanguine is naturally friendly and open to those under their leadership or at home. They will likely want everyone to be their friend. They usually take a team approach to management wanting everyone to cooperate. The Sanguine is easy to follow because they naturally communicate acceptance to others. They may have difficulty when they need to confront someone.

Eating Habits

The Sanguine tends to view food as a celebration. They enjoy the event of eating with others; life is a party to the Sanguine. Once the party gets started they exercise little restraint and will likely overeat. Of course, some with the Sanguine temperament will control their eating habits driven by their need to have an acceptable appearance in the eyes of others.

Sleep

The Sanguine temperament blends varies widely in the amount of sleep that is necessary (depends on their second temperament). For example, the Sanguine-Choleric usually needs around seven hours, the Sanguine-Phlegmatic needs at least eight (or more), and the Sanguine-Melancholy can operate on three-five hours (even less) if they are in a creative mood.

As a Mate

The Sanguine is the most affectionate of the four temperaments. They require a lot of touch, affection, and interaction from their mate.

The Sanguine is flexible, spontaneous, impulsive, and talkative — this may require a lot of patience from their mate.

They like to be on the go or around people most of the time. Do not expect them to just sit and watch the world go by — they are not spectators, they are participants in life. The Sanguine likes sports and outside activities. They are so people-oriented that they often forget about time because they are enjoying themselves; this of course, can cause tension with their mate because of not being where they are supposed to be ... on time. They may to do things to excess.

The Sanguine can be very romantic and they enjoy celebrating just about anything. The Sanguine is usually so fun-oriented that it takes a patient, tolerant, understanding mate to be in a successful relationship with them. These tendencies will be modified depending on the influence of the second temperament and their maturity level.

How Would a Sanguine Control or Manage Their Family?

Sanguines are typically social, outgoing, and enthusiastic. They usually have a positive and cheerful disposition. There will be some differences of how a Sanguine influences or manages their family based on their second temperament. While they may not be controlling or authoritarian, they tend to influence their family dynamics in a more subtle, persuasive, and energetic way. In general, here's how a Sanguine might control or manage their family, the Sanguine will likely ...

1. ... be very charming and have a magnetic personality. Their charm helps them persuade family members to agree with their ideas or suggestions. They often use their lively energy to get people on their side, making their family members feel comfortable and happy around them. This creates a sense of warmth, unity, and acceptance.

2. ... use positive reinforcement. They encourage family members by emphasizing the good behavior and celebrating successes.

3. ... keep a family motivated and optimistic during tough times. Their energetic and positive outlook often leads them to take on the role of problem solver or cheerleader within the family. In this way, they indirectly take control of situations by uplifting others and steering the emotional tone of the family.

4. ... maintain social connections. They can build strong networks, including family bonds, by keeping everyone in touch and making events or family gatherings enjoyable. Through their ability to entertain and bring people together, they influence the social dynamics within the family.

5. ... dislike conflict and prefer to keep things lighthearted. They may use humor to diffuse tension within the family, thus ensuring a harmonious environment where they do not need to assert control forcefully. Instead, they encourage cooperation through acceptance and laughter.

6. ... take control of family events or social activities, filling the household with excitement and joy. They can be the life of the party.

7. ... be able to relate to their family members and can adapt their communication style to connect with them on a deeper level. This makes them more influential in steering family decisions or resolving conflicts.

Challenges: Though Sanguines are great at connecting with others, they might sometimes lack attention to detail or consistency in rules and boundaries, which could lead to challenges in maintaining control over more structured or routine aspects of family life. Nonetheless, their persuasive and charismatic nature often compensates for these weaknesses.

In conclusion, a Sanguine usually influences their family not by authoritarian control but through their charisma, positive attitude, and social abilities. They guide and influence the family dynamic by fostering positivity, connection, and harmony, often taking on a leadership role in family activities and social interactions.

Chapter 5

THE PERFORMER
Sanguine-Melancholy

The Performer is a combination of the Sanguine temperament being first and the Melancholy temperament being second. Your primary motivation is to be *accepted* socially. Your secondary motivation is to *do things right.* Either motivation may dominate your behavior depending on the requirements of the situation.

Performer Pattern

When the Sanguine and the Melancholy natural tendencies are combined, it produces a people-person who is sensitive, creative, and detail-oriented. The Sanguine-Melancholy is more emotional and can be more formal acting than the other Sanguine blends. This combination is naturally able to *perform* in front of others to meet the need of the moment. The Sanguine-Melancholy is a frequently found pattern and the most visible in society.

Description

As a Sanguine-Melancholy you need to be with people *most* of the time but *some* of the time you need to be alone. When alone you will likely think, review, plan, or express your creativity.

You need information, time to think, and a plan; you function best, and more effectively when you have a detailed plan. Once you have a plan, however, you may struggle to be consistent or follow through because of the fear of failure. Once the fear of failure is overcome there is not much you cannot do as well, if not better than, anyone else.

As a Sanguine-Melancholy you have a very active, vivid imagination which enables you to be creative in many areas like music, the performing arts, writing, decoration, problem solving, etc. You tend to be image conscious and actively seek recognition for your achievements. You have a deep need to know that you are accepted by others. You may struggle with questions like "Why did I do that?" or "Why didn't I do something else?" or "Did I say that right?"

You are usually well organized. Being organized does not necessarily mean that everything is neatly in place. Being organized can also mean that you know where everything is located — if you know what's in the piles then you're organized!

Information about your job is very important to you so you may ask many questions before accepting a task. You tend to be cautious because of your need to make a favorable impression. You like status and quality things.

25

You often have difficulty going to sleep because you are reviewing your day, planning tomorrow, fretting, or creating. Your emotions may fluctuate, especially if you are embarrassed or you have been, or may be, rejected. You can do things to an extreme. You tend to warm up slowly to new people. Once you feel comfortable, you open up and become more friendly.

Strengths

Creative ability Your greatest strength is your *creative ability*; your temperament blend is the most creative of all the other combinations. Your creativity can be in art, music, problem solving, etc. You tend to have great writing ability that shows up in stories, poetry, and writing songs. You tend to have speaking ability too. The Sanguine part presents well what your Melancholy side has thought through .

High drive to win You are capable of persuading others with facts and emotion. You are driven to do a task correctly and make a good impression in the process. You are capable of being the top in your chosen field.

Weaknesses

As a Sanguine-Melancholy you may struggle controlling your *thoughts* and *emotions*. Uncontrolled, your thoughts can be so extreme and so overwhelming that you think you are unable to control what you think about (which is not true as you will see later). You are naturally capable of feeling so deeply that you become overwhelmed and consumed by your emotions. You may think you are incapable of feeling okay again.

As a Sanguine-Melancholy you were born with the entire range of human emotions. You are capable of getting more excited than anyone (the top of emotion) and you are capable of getting more down than anyone (the bottom of emotion).

Sensitive Since you have a fear of being rejected you tend to be very sensitive to the way others respond to you. You can be offended over the slightest thing and may react emotionally.

Emotional highs and lows You can have emotional highs and lows fueled by being rejected and/or failure to spend sufficient alone time.

Extreme emotion You are capable of expressing intense emotion, become critical and condescending and/or get verbally (sometimes physically) aggressive. This may be followed (but not always) by remorse and lengthy periods of isolation. Fears associated with your temperament blend are listed below.

Mood Shifts

There are two reasons why: 1) Your are not getting enough alone time. You enjoy being with, by, or near, someone else *most* of the time which satisfies the Sanguine part. But you also need to spend time alone *some* of the time which satisfies the Melancholy part. Once your daily need to be with people has been met a switch flips which signals you're ready to be away from people for some alone time. The amount of time needed varies with each person. Once that need is met another switch flips and you're ready to be around people again. If you neglect spending time alone everyday you will be irritated and uneasy around people until you are able to be alone. This "shift in your mood" is normal and natural. This is not a weakness but a normal functioning of your temperament blend. The need to be alone is normal, natural, and necessary! 2) A second reason for a *mood shift* is you have been, or you think you may be, rejected, or made to look unfavorable in the eyes of others. The *mood shift* here represents a need to withdraw to deal with the emotional pain you are feeling. How to deal with the fear of being rejected is addressed later in this workbook.

Needs
As a Sanguine-Melancholy your effectiveness in relationships and productivity in your career may be hindered because of your temperament needs not being met. Your natural temperament needs include being with people socially, spending adequate time alone, and having a plan. The amount of daily alone time needed varies with the individual. You also need a variety of activities because you tend to get bored easily and often once you've figured out the challenge. When these natural needs are *not* met you will experience increased anxiety and noticeable shifts in your mood.

Fears
Fear tends to create anger. *Fear* is a primary emotion and *anger* is a secondary emotion. You may respond with extreme emotion if any of your natural fears are realized (or you think they may be realized), such as: being rejected, losing or failing, being embarrassed (especially in public), being criticized personally, being slighted, not doing the task correctly, not making a favorable impression, not being successful, or being disrespected. You may be reluctant to start a new project until you have confidence that you will not fail. If you are not sure that you will succeed you may not try. You tend to ask lots of specific questions to avoid failure or being embarrassed.

Response to Pressure
When under pressure or stress, you may react with strong emotions and become angry and critical. You may release your frustration by talking, withdrawing, attacking verbally, or becoming depressed. You may deny the reality of the situation and try to manipulate others to your point of view with intense emotion.

Causes of Procrastination
You may procrastinate if you think that you may not make a favorable impression or if the risk of failure is too great. You may be unsure of the right way to accomplish the task without failing. You may also forget to do what you promised.

Different Expressions of the Sanguine-Melancholy Blend
People are infinitely complex. No two individuals will behave the same even with the same temperament blend. There are three major levels of expression listed below. These levels are fixed and do not change over a person's lifespan. What changes is whether or not a person uses their natural strengths and overcomes the negative impact of their natural weaknesses. The Sanguine is driven, at all three levels, to be socially active and accepted to some degree. The Sanguine does not need a reason to be around other people.

Unlike other temperament combinations, the Sanguine-Melancholy has the natural ability to express the entire range of human emotions. The Sanguine can get more *excited* than the other temperaments and the Melancholy can get *further down* than the other temperaments. Because of their emotional range they will differ widely in expression and behavior more than any other temperament combination.

Level 1 - Narrow

This means the *influence* of the *second* temperament (Melancholy) is ***not far from*** the first temperament (Sanguine): **Sanguine → Melancholy**. In this alignment, the Melancholy traits have significant impact on behavior. The closer these two temperaments are to each other the more competition there is between the two for expression in behavior.

In this alignment, the Melancholy is *very* close to the Sanguine which means that less Sanguine tendencies will be expressed and more of the Melancholy tendencies will be observed in normal, everyday behavior. This person will smile less, be more serious, and be more subtly in social activity.

They will be a more cautious and guarded person (they often see themselves as introverted). This close proximity of the Melancholy to the Sanguine means the individual can easily move from showing Sanguine tendencies to showing Melancholy tendencies. They will plan in more detail and be more analytical about most everything. This person will need lots of alone time. This combination will act more formal in public.

Level 2 - Moderate

The spread between the Sanguine and Melancholy is enough to allow the Melancholy tendencies to be expressed and easily seen in interaction with others: **Sanguine → → Melancholy**. In this alignment the Sanguine tendencies of friendliness are easily observed with frequent smiles. The Melancholy tendencies of being cautious and careful around others is also noticeable.

Level 3 - Wide

This means that there is a *significant* separation of the *second* temperament (Melancholy) from the *first* temperament (Sanguine): **Sanguine → → → Melancholy**. In this alignment, the more the Melancholy is *separated* from the Sanguine, the more Sanguine tendencies will be visible in behavior. This person will be openly friendly, excitable, and talk more. The primary Sanguine temperament will be more *intensely* expressed the greater the separation from the Melancholy (second) temperament. This person can get *very* excited about people and events.

Influence of the third and fourth temperaments:

The combination of the Sanguine and Melancholy temperaments *allows* for the Choleric and Phlegmatic tendencies to influence behavior.

A. When the **Choleric** is third, the person will be more direct in conversation. When suddenly direct or blunt they may be offensive to others. Since the Phlegmatic is the *fourth* (and least) tendency, this person will also be less predictable, more impulsive, and less emotionally stable.

B. When the **Phlegmatic** is third, this person will be less direct and more pleasant. This is the most frequently occurring alignment of the Sanguine-Melancholy combination. This person will have difficult confronting others since the Choleric is the *fourth* (and least) tendency.

Note: The closeness (proximity) of the *second* temperament, Melancholy, to the *primary* temperament, Sanguine, makes the biggest difference in how this combination is expressed in normal, natural behavior.

The combination of Sanguine-Melancholy produces a push/pull within the person. This natural *tug-of-war* causes confusion for the one with this combination. The Sanguine is *pulling* the person to be *with* people and the Melancholy is *pushing* the person to be alone.

Sanguine-Melancholy Strengths

A. Your Evaluation

Check ✓ all that represent your behavior and rate each one on a scale of one to ten:

☐ Sociable   Like Me 10—9—8—7—6—5—4—3—2—1 Not Like Me

☐ Creative   Like Me 10—9—8—7—6—5—4—3—2—1 Not Like Me

☐ Likes to do things right   Like Me 10—9—8—7—6—5—4—3—2—1 Not Like Me

☐ High drive to win   Like Me 10—9—8—7—6—5—4—3—2—1 Not Like Me

☐ Initiates projects   Like Me 10—9—8—7—6—5—4—3—2—1 Not Like Me

☐ Articulate   Like Me 10—9—8—7—6—5—4—3—2—1 Not Like Me

☐ Persuades with facts and emotions   Like Me 10—9—8—7—6—5—4—3—2—1 Not Like Me

☐ Seeks social influence   Like Me 10—9—8—7—6—5—4—3—2—1 Not Like Me

☐ Problem solver   Like Me 10—9—8—7—6—5—4—3—2—1 Not Like Me

1. How aware are you of your natural strengths?

       Aware   10—9—8—7—6—5—4—3—2—1   Not Aware

2. List three strengths that you appreciate the most about yourself?

   _____

   _____

   _____

3. How can expressing these strengths in a controlled manner help you be more effective?

   _____

   _____

4. On the next page: ask someone who knows you well (mate, family member, friend, etc.) to check ✓ all that represent your behavior and ask them to rate each one on a scale of one to ten.

Sanguine-Melancholy Strengths

B. Second Evaluation by:

Name _____ Date _____

Check ✓ all that represent the behavior of the person you are evaluating and rate each one on a scale of one to ten:

☐ Sociable   Like Me 10—9—8—7—6—5—4—3—2—1 Not Like Me

☐ Creative   Like Me 10—9—8—7—6—5—4—3—2—1 Not Like Me

☐ Likes to do things right   Like Me 10—9—8—7—6—5—4—3—2—1 Not Like Me

☐ High drive to win   Like Me 10—9—8—7—6—5—4—3—2—1 Not Like Me

☐ Initiates projects   Like Me 10—9—8—7—6—5—4—3—2—1 Not Like Me

☐ Articulate   Like Me 10—9—8—7—6—5—4—3—2—1 Not Like Me

☐ Persuades with facts and emotions   Like Me 10—9—8—7—6—5—4—3—2—1 Not Like Me

☐ Seeks social influence   Like Me 10—9—8—7—6—5—4—3—2—1 Not Like Me

☐ Problem solver   Like Me 10—9—8—7—6—5—4—3—2—1 Not Like Me

Compare the choices you made with the person that did the same. Answer the following:

1. Was the evaluation the same?   ☐ Yes ☐ No

2. Discuss the agreement or disagreement.

3. What did you learn from this exercise?

_____

4. What do you need to improve?

_____

_____

The Sanguine-Melancholy's Positive Impact on Others

As a Sanguine-Melancholy you have a natural, positive impact on others. Check ✓ all that apply from the following list:

☐ Creative thinking   Like Me 10—9—8—7—6—5—4—3—2—1 Not Like Me

☐ Ptoduces creative works   Like Me 10—9—8—7—6—5—4—3—2—1 Not Like Me

☐ Good speaker   Like Me 10—9—8—7—6—5—4—3—2—1 Not Like Me

☐ Needs to gather information   Like Me 10—9—8—7—6—5—4—3—2—1 Not Like Me

☐ Needs to analyze   Like Me 10—9—8—7—6—5—4—3—2—1 Not Like Me

☐ Sociable   Like Me 10—9—8—7—6—5—4—3—2—1 Not Like Me

☐ Social influencer   Like Me 10—9—8—7—6—5—4—3—2—1 Not Like Me

Which one has the greatest impact on others?

_____

Which one do you need to use/develop more?

_____

How will you use/develop the one you chose?

_____

_____

_____

_____

Sanguine-Melancholy Weaknesses

A. Your Evaluation

☐ Impulsive   Like Me 10—9—8—7—6—5—4—3—2—1 Not Like Me

☐ Inconsistent   Like Me 10—9—8—7—6—5—4—3—2—1 Not Like Me

☐ Talks too much   Like Me 10—9—8—7—6—5—4—3—2—1 Not Like Me

☐ Plays too much   Like Me 10—9—8—7—6—5—4—3—2—1 Not Like Me

☐ Thinks too much about the wrong thing Like Me 10—9—8—7—6—5—4—3—2—1 Not Like Me

☐ Too sensitive   Like Me 10—9—8—7—6—5—4—3—2—1 Not Like Me

☐ Emotions may fluctuate   Like Me 10—9—8—7—6—5—4—3—2—1 Not Like Me

☐ Unrealistic standards   Like Me 10—9—8—7—6—5—4—3—2—1 Not Like Me

☐ Fears rejection; image conscious Like Me 10—9—8—7—6—5—4—3—2—1 Not Like Me

☐ Condescending; bite in voice   Like Me 10—9—8—7—6—5—4—3—2—1 Not Like Me

☐ May do things to extreme   Like Me 10—9—8—7—6—5—4—3—2—1 Not Like Me

1. How aware are you of these natural weaknesses?

       Aware   10—9—8—7—6—5—4—3—2—1   Not Aware

2. List one weakness that you would like to overcome.

      _____

3. How does this weakness interfere with your effectiveness in your daily life?

      _____

4. How would your relationships improve if you developed a plan to control and overcome the negative impact of your weaknesses?

      ☐ I would be more effective   ☐ Stress will be reduced

      ☐ I would be better received by others   ☐ Communication with others will improve

5. On the next page: ask someone who knows you well (mate, family member, friend, etc.) to check all that represent your behavior and ask them to rate each one on a scale of one to ten.

Sanguine-Melancholy Weaknesses

B. Second Evaluation by:

Name _____ Date _____

Check ✓ all that represent the behavior of the person you are evaluating and rate each one on a scale of one to ten:

☐ Impulsive   Like Me 10—9—8—7—6—5—4—3—2—1 Not Like Me

☐ Inconsistent   Like Me 10—9—8—7—6—5—4—3—2—1 Not Like Me

☐ Talks too much   Like Me 10—9—8—7—6—5—4—3—2—1 Not Like Me

☐ Plays too much   Like Me 10—9—8—7—6—5—4—3—2—1 Not Like Me

☐ Thinks too much about the wrong thing Like Me 10—9—8—7—6—5—4—3—2—1 Not Like Me

☐ Too sensitive   Like Me 10—9—8—7—6—5—4—3—2—1 Not Like Me

☐ Emotions may fluctuate   Like Me 10—9—8—7—6—5—4—3—2—1 Not Like Me

☐ Unrealistic standards   Like Me 10—9—8—7—6—5—4—3—2—1 Not Like Me

☐ Fears rejection; image conscious   Like Me 10—9—8—7—6—5—4—3—2—1 Not Like Me

☐ Condescending; bite in voice   Like Me 10—9—8—7—6—5—4—3—2—1 Not Like Me

☐ May do things to extreme   Like Me 10—9—8—7—6—5—4—3—2—1 Not Like Me

Compare the choices you make with the person that did the same. Answer the following:

1. Was agreement close to the same?   ☐ Yes ☐ No
2. Discuss the differences if any.
3. What did you learn from this exercise?

_____

_____

_____

_____

How To Deal With Weaknesses

All temperament blends have *natural* strengths and weaknesses. However, a strength overextended will become a weakness. Your lack of self-control will cause the weaknesses listed above.

To overcome any weakness you must first become **aware** that it is something you do, take **ownership** of what you are doing, and then **decide** to **change** your thinking and behavior.

> **Romans 12:2** *And do not be conformed to this world, but be transformed by the renewing of your mind* (see pages 61-62).

•*Change Your Thinking.* This passage teaches that you have to *change* what you have been thinking and doing. You do that by *renewing* your mind. The word *renewing* means to *renovate* (when you renovate something you take out old and replace it with new). So, when you *renovate* your mind you take out *old* thinking and behavior and replace it with *new* thinking and behavior. The old thinking and behavior that shows weaknesses has to *stop* and be replaced with *new* thinking and behavior that comes from the Bible.

•*Use Self-Control.* Once the decision is made to change you now must engage in redirecting or re-programming your thoughts, feelings, and behavior by using self-control. Every book in the New Testament includes instructions like *put on, put off, start, stop.* All the writers encouraged self-control to *stop* certain behavior and start better behavior. This is a process that takes time to gain mastery over your thoughts, feelings, behavior, desires, speech, and impulses (see pages 63-66).

> **Ephesians 4:22-24** *that you **put off**, concerning your former conduct, the old man which grows corrupt according to the deceitful lusts, 23 and be renewed in the spirit of your mind, 24 and that you **put on** the new man which was created according to God, in true righteousness and holiness.*

> **Galatians 5:22-23** *But the fruit of the Spirit is love, joy, peace, longsuffering, kindness, goodness, faithfulness, gentleness, **self-control**.*

> **Proverbs 16:32** *Better a patient person than a warrior, one with **self-control** than one who takes a city.*

The contrast in Proverbs 16:32 is between having great *physical strength* verses having *self-control*. First, you are far better to be patient (slow to anger) than one who is physically very strong. Second, if you control your spirit or temper, you are better than one who can capture a city. The idea is that you are so physically strong that you not only *capture* a city but you alone can *keep* the city under your control!

Issues you may struggle with are listed below with suggestions on how to overcome the negative impact they may be having in your life.

1. Impulsive. Being impulsive can make life interesting and fun ... when it is harmless. But when you are recklessly impulsive it's a sign of immaturity and shows a lack of wisdom. When recklessly impulsive you run the risk of making rash decisions, having risky behaviors, and saying things you wish you had not said. A rash decision could be financially harmful too. Impulsive behavior is a self-control issue (see pages 63-66).

> **Proverbs 25:28** *Whoever has no rule over his own spirit is like a city broken down, without walls.*

This verse is teaching that impulsive actions leaves a person vulnerable and unprotected like a city without walls. The Bible encourages thoughtful decision-making rather than quick, rash actions. Slow down, be patient, and carefully consider the consequences of your decision. **James 1:19-20** advises, *Everyone should be quick to listen, slow to speak and slow to become angry, because human anger does not produce the righteousness that God desires.* This verse encourages taking time to reflect and listen before acting which may avoid impulsive decisions and negative consequences.

☐ I will consider the consequences before I act.

2. Need to be important. A phenomenon that many with the Sanguine-Melancholy temperament struggle with is the *need to be important*. To understand this struggle consider these five elements:

A. The Sanguine part has a natural drive to seek approval and attention from others. They tend to thrive in environments where they are noticed and celebrated and enjoy being the center of attention. This trait produces a strong desire to feel important in social settings or in relationships.. They frequently seek recognition or validation from others to feel valued and seen.

B. The Melancholy part is both introspective and perfectionistic. The Melancholy part is very analytical and has a high drive to figure out what *is* right (not trying to *be* right).

C. Both possess strong emotions. The Sanguine part can produce extreme excitement and the Melancholy part can produce deep feelings of sadness.

D. The Sanguine-Melancholy tends to have a higher IQ and the ability to process lots of information quickly.

E. The Sanguine-Melancholy is gifted and creative. Their creativity is often seen in problem solving, art, music, singing, acting, dancing, writing, teaching, medicine, inventing, sports, beauty pageants, etc. The Sanguine-Melancholy, therefore, is quite capable of achieving great success in their area of interest. What may prevent success is giving in to the fear of failure causing one to not even try.

Every ability a person has comes from God. **James 1:17** states, *Every good gift and every perfect gift is from above, and comes down from the Father of lights, with whom there is no variation or shadow of turning.* If you, as a Sanguine-Melancholy, fail to understand this, you will take pride in your abilities. What does the Bible say about that?

Proverbs 11:2 *When pride comes, then comes disgrace, but with humility comes wisdom.*

Proverbs 16:5 *The LORD detests all the proud of heart. Be sure of this: They will not go unpunished.*

Proverbs 16:18 *Pride goes before destruction, And a haughty spirit before a fall.*

Proverbs 27:1-2 *Do not boast about tomorrow, For you do not know what a day may bring forth. 2 Let another man praise you, and not your own mouth; A stranger, and not your own lips.*

Romans 12:3 *For I say, through the grace given to me, to everyone who is among you, not to think of himself more highly than he ought to think, but to think soberly, as God has dealt to each one a measure of faith.*

People who are overconfident or arrogant are likely to fail. If this is your issue realize that God has given you the intellect and abilities you possess. Do not boast about what you have and do not praise yourself. Give thanks to God. Do not draw attention to yourself by boasting about your abilities or accomplishments. Give God the glory.

☐ I will give glory to God for what He has given me.
☐ I will not draw attention to myself.
☐ I will not boast about my accomplishments.

3. May Talk Too Much. You typically have a lot to say. Be aware that at times you may talk too much. Also, your voice may be louder than others. Just be aware that if you're talking to someone, and others are around, your voice may carry too far and disturb other conversations. This proverb cautions you to be aware and regulate how much you talk.

Proverbs 10:19 *In the multitude of words sin is not lacking, But he who restrains his lips is wise.*

Check ✓ if you're willing to work on controlling how much (and how loud) you talk.

☐ I am aware that I may talk too much at times.

☐ I am aware that I may talk too loud at times.

4. Edge in voice. Be aware that your tone of voice can have a *bite* in it. Having a *bite in your voice* means that you show a little *irritation* in the way you are speaking. The *bite* actually represents anger and discuss. Love doesn't act this way. Here are a few ways that love behaves **I Corinthians 13:4-8** (for a full list see pages 83-84):

•Love is patient - love never takes the opportunity to avenge itself.
•Love is kind - love never offends, insults or says anything unkind.
•Love is not rude - love has good manners and makes you feel comfortable.
•Love seeks not it's own - love does not trade being right for another person's feelings.
•Love is not provoked - love does not get irritated.

A Summary of I Corinthians 13:4-8 by Dr. Tom Constable:
Love does not deal with other people in a way that injures their dignity. It does not insist on having its own way, nor does it put its own interest before the needs of others. Love is not irritable or touchy, and it **absorbs** offenses, insults, and inconveniences for the sake of others' welfare. It does not keep a record of offenses received to pay them back.

☐ I will love people like this.

How To Deal With Fears

The first negative emotion experience by Adam and Eve was the *fear* that God would find out what they had done, Genesis 3:8-10. So now, through Adam, we are all fearful. Here is, perhaps, your greatest fear:

Fear of Rejection. The core fear of your Sanguine-Melancholy blend is the fear of being rejected. This fear is an intense anxiety about being criticized, judged, making a bad impression, making a mistake, being excluded by others, being disrespected, losing, being viewed as unsuccessful, etc.

The fear of rejection is such a powerful feeling that it can be overwhelming and even paralyzing. This fear is part of the natural tendencies of the Sanguine-Melancholy blend with which you were born. Rate your level of agreement of a fear of rejection on a scale of one to ten:

Like Me 10—9—8—7—6—5—4—3—2—1 Not Like Me

Why does the Sanguine-Melancholy temperament naturally fear being rejected? Let's review. It is a combination of two different temperaments that are both opposite and opposing. The Sanguine part is social, lively, optimistic, and wants to be with people. Whereas the Melancholy part is introspective, perfectionistic, sensitive, and wants to be alone. This combination produces one who can be eager to connect with others but also deeply aware of personal flaws or potential for failure. An examination of this combination helps to explain why there is a natural fear of rejection with which you were born.

1. Desire for social connection: The Sanguine part wants social interaction and approval. Rejection can feel like a direct threat to your sense of belonging or value, making you sensitive to being rejected.
2. Self-criticism: The Melancholy part tends to be highly self-critical, and this can lead to self-rejection. You may fear rejection not just because of other people's opinion but because you have already deeply examined yourself. The thought of being rejected can feel like confirmation of your conclusions.
3. Perfectionism: The Melancholy part has high standards for themselves and others. You may fear rejection because you feel you must meet certain expectations to be worthy of acceptance.
4. Emotional vulnerability: The Sanguine-Melancholy temperament is deeply emotional so rejection feels not just like a social setback but like a personal attack.
5. Contradiction between traits: The Sanguine part wants to be loved and accepted by others, while the Melancholy part is prone to withdrawing and self-doubt. This internal contradiction can make you fear rejection even more as you oscillate between wanting to be accepted and feeling inadequate.

The Scripture says two things about your existence:

1. You are made in the *image* of God. Genesis 1:27 states *So God created man in His own image, in the image of God created He him; male and female He created them.* The word "image" means *resemblance* which means we resemble God because we can think, feel, and choose.
2. You are unique. Psalm 139:14 states we are *fearfully and wonderfully made. Wonderfully* in Hebrew means unique and set apart. The verse teaches that each person is a unique work of art created by God. For these reasons do not be critical of yourself.

Reactions to what has happened, or what may happen, may include an extreme emotional response, being verbally unkind, physically abusive, or withdrawal to fume about what happened. You may avoid similar situations in the future to prevent the same feelings from occurring. You may also avoid initiating or participating in social activities to prevent the possibility of rejection.

Giving in to the possibility of being rejected or losing may cause you to not try to do something or make significant changes to avoid the possibility of failing. This fear could cause you to redirect your career path, and if not overcome, will stop you from pursuing your potential.

Are you making decisions that would reduce the possibility of failing? Has your fear of failing prevented you from pursuing what you really want to do or be in life? Is it possible to overcome this fear to pursue the things you would like to accomplish? The answer is yes!

What does the Bible say about the fear of rejection? The Bible does not have a specific verse about fearing rejection but it does address fear.

1.   Christians are commanded not to fear throughout the Bible. Actually it is the most repeated command in the Bible. There are at least 365 occurrences of *fear not* in the Bible, one for each day! God wants you to want what He wants. God wants you be willing to accept the outcome of anything you are trying to do as coming from Him. When you fear that you will not get what you want you are bypassing what God is doing in your life.

2.   When you fear rejection you are placing too much importance on yourself (pride).

> **Romans 12:3** *For I say, through the grace given to me, to everyone who is among you, **not to think of himself more highly than he ought to think**, but to think soberly, as God has dealt to each one a measure of faith.*

3.   When you fear rejection you are placing too much importance on what other people think.

> **I Corinthians 4:3** *But with me **it is a very small thing** that I should be judged by you or by a human court.*

4.   When you fear rejection you are leaving God out of the *situation* that's causing the fear. The purpose of the Christian life is to be conformed into the image of His Son. So, all things that happen in your life have a purpose, even experiencing rejection. This means that God doesn't do anything **to** you, He does it **for** you (see page 57).

> **Romans 8:28-29** *And we know that all things work together for good to those who love God, to those who are the called according to His purpose. 29 For whom He foreknew, He also predestined to be conformed to the image of His Son, that He might be the firstborn among many brethren.*

5.   When you are anxious and do not take your concern to the Lord, you're leaving Him out of the *solution*. Being anxious means that you are mentally and emotionally concerned that the outcome may not be favorable and your image may be tarnished. Paul ***commands*** us not to be anxious but rather tell the Lord about your concerns and give Him thanks for the event and accept whatever He does. When you do that He promises to give you peace that you cannot comprehend. The peace that God grants to you will protect you from experiencing overwhelming emotions and thoughts (see pages 73-74).

> **Philippians 4:6-7** *Be anxious for nothing, but in everything by prayer and supplication, with thanksgiving, let your requests be made known to God; 7 and the peace of God, which surpasses all understanding, will guard your hearts and minds through Christ Jesus.*

> **I Peter 5:7** *Cast all your care* [anxiety] *on him because he cares for you.*

Thank God for using the event and giving you peace that protects your emotions and thoughts. Do not take it personal and do not react with strong emotions or negative thoughts. Let God work in your situation. The more you do this the stronger you will become to reduce and eliminate the negative impact of anxiety in your life. If you continue to work hard not to allow these events to cause you mental and emotional pain you will be able to do as King David did. Here is what happen when he was rejected and how he responded as recorded in II Samuel 16:5-14:

King David lived over three thousand years ago and was the greatest ruler of Israel. He wrote more than half of the Psalms including Psalms 23 which is the most read piece of literature of all time. He was a Sanguine-Melancholy and he records in the Psalms his emotional ups and downs. He battled many fears including the fear of rejection. Here's the incident that reveals the best way to handle being rejected.

> Now when King David came to Bahurim, there was a man from the family of the house of Saul, whose name was Shimei the son of Gera, coming from there. He came out, cursing continuously as he came. 6 And he threw stones at David and at all the servants of King David. And all the people and all the mighty men were on his right hand and on his left. 7 Also Shimei said thus when he cursed: "Come out! Come out! You bloodthirsty man, you rogue! 8 The Lord has brought upon you all the blood of the house of Saul, in whose place you have reigned; and the Lord has delivered the kingdom into the hand of Absalom your son. So now you are caught in your own evil, because you are a bloodthirsty man!" 9 Then Abishai the son of Zeruiah said to the king, "Why should this dead dog curse my lord the king? Please, let me go over and take off his head!"10 But the king said, "What have I to do with you, you sons of Zeruiah? So let him curse, because the Lord has said to him, 'Curse David.' Who then shall say, 'Why have you done so?' "11 And David said to Abishai and all his servants, "See how my son who came from my own body seeks my life. How much more now may this Benjamite? Let him alone, and let him curse; for so the Lord has ordered him. 12 It may be

that the Lord will look on [d]my affliction, and that the Lord will repay me with good for his cursing this day." 13 And as David and his men went along the road, Shimei went along the hillside opposite him and cursed as he went, threw stones at him and kicked up dust. 14 Now the king and all the people who were with him became weary; so they refreshed themselves there.

To say David was disliked by Shimei is an understatement! He despised David and all that he stood for. But David did not take it personal. He believed God was involved in the event. This is the only way to deal with the possibility of being rejected or slighted in some way. In every incident God wants you to trust Him. Let God work in these moments to conform you into the image of His Son.

What would your life look like if you overcame the fear of rejection? You can be whatever you set your mind to achieving as long it's within your level of expertise (you cannot fly without wings or an airplane!). But you can work toward achieving your ability if you overcome the fear that may be preventing you from trying.

I worked with a sales company that had around 600 salespeople. I taught how to use the temperament model of behavior in selling every month for five years. Here's what happened:

> The majority of sale people hired were Sanguine-Melancholy. It was a three week training period that ended on a Saturday. The salespeople traveled back to their respective cities on Sunday to begin work on Monday. They were required to call prospects to set up appointments to attempt a sale. All they had to do was dial the phone and call a prospect. Most of the Sanguine-Melancholies would not even attempt to make a call! They were afraid they would not get an appointment. So most failed within the first two weeks! However, the Sanguine-Melancholy that was afraid they would not get the appointment called more prospects than they were asked to do! It was a Sanguine-Melancholy that broke the record every time for first month selling!

A friend of mine ask me to talk to his friend who was failing at his sales job.

> He was in an industry that paid a huge commission for a sale (up to six figures). I pointed out that his issue was that he was afraid to ask for the order more than once. I validated that he was Sanguine-Melancholy and that he was giving in to the fear of failing by giving up too quickly. He accepted that was his issue and decided to "face the fear and not give up!" Within three days he made a sale and made the huge commission!

You have a choice to make. You can continue to let the fear of anything like that of rejection, failing, etc., to control your life or you can begin to work at overcoming the impact it has on your life and future. The journey of a thousand mile begins with the first step. Take this step and see what your life can become.

Guidelines to help you face and overcome fear:

A. <u>Acknowledge God's Presence</u>. The Bible reminds us that we are never alone, and God is always with us. When fear arises, remember that God's presence is with you, and He will give you the strength to face any challenge.

> Isaiah 41:10 So do not fear, for I am with you; do not be dismayed, for I am your God.
> I will strengthen you and help you; I will uphold you with my righteous right hand.

B. <u>Trust in God's Sovereignty</u>. Understanding that God is in control of all circumstances can help relieve fear. Fear stems from a sense of uncertainty but knowing that God is sovereign reassures us that He is in control of everything.

> Psalm 34:4 I sought the Lord, and he answered me; he delivered me from all my fears.

> Romans 8:28 And we know that in all things God works for the good of those who love him, who have been called according to his purpose.

> 1 Thessalonians 5:18 in everything give thanks; for this is the will of God in Christ Jesus for you.

> Trust that no matter what happens, God is working for your good.

C. <u>Cast Your Cares on God</u>. Instead of letting fear overwhelm you, take your concerns directly to God in prayer. He cares for you and wants to carry your burdens. This act of surrender helps release the grip of fear and anxiety.

> 1 Peter 5:7 *Cast all your anxiety on him because he cares for you.*

D. <u>Change your thinking</u> from "I am afraid" to I am not afraid." I know that's not so easy to do so the next time you are fearful of something quote **Proverbs 3:5-6:**

> *Trust in the Lord with all your heart, And lean not on your own understanding;*
> *6 In all your ways acknowledge Him, And He shall direct your paths.*

Do not leave God out of what is happening. Thank God for using the event to help conform you into Christ's image. Check ✓ what you will do to overcome the negative impact fear is having in your life:

- ☐ I will not be fearful of what may or may not happen.
- ☐ I will trust God no matter what happens (see pages 59-60).

Sanguine-Melancholy Tendencies Needed For Balance

In order to be a more balanced person, as a Sanguine-Melancholy, you need to incorporate *tendencies* from both the Choleric and Phlegmatic temperaments into your behavior.

To this point, the focus has been on the primary and the secondary temperaments that make up your temperament combination. You are, however, a blend of all four temperaments. You can be either Sanguine-Melancholy-**Phlegmatic**-Choleric or Sanguine-Melancholy-**Choleric**-Phlegmatic. The most common blend is the Phlegmatic being third.

Regardless of the natural position of the Choleric and Phlegmatic temperaments become comfortable with expressing either tendency when the need arises. Adding the tendencies of the third and fourth temperaments will enable you to have a balanced approach to dealing with others and the circumstances of life.

Check ✓ all the needs below that you feel would complement your temperament combination and is lacking in your behavior. Rate your level of need on a scale of one to ten:

☐ Control of emotions   Needed 10—9—8—7—6—5—4—3—2—1 Not needed

☐ Consistent effort and follow through   Needed 10—9—8—7—6—5—4—3—2—1 Not needed

☐ Realistic standards / goals   Needed 10—9—8—7—6—5—4—3—2—1 Not needed

☐ More directness   Needed 10—9—8—7—6—5—4—3—2—1 Not needed

☐ Overcoming fears   Needed 10—9—8—7—6—5—4—3—2—1 Not needed

☐ Self-control   Needed 10—9—8—7—6—5—4—3—2—1 Not needed

☐ Sufficient alone time   Needed 10—9—8—7—6—5—4—3—2—1 Not needed

☐ Positive self-talk   Needed 10—9—8—7—6—5—4—3—2—1 Not needed

The four temperaments represent *different* ways of approaching people and events. In a given situation a tendency from another temperament may be more effective and efficient. The key is to be flexible and willing to function in any of the four temperament tendencies when it is necessary.

For example, as a Sanguine-Melancholy, you may struggle with consistency, whereas, the Phlegmatic tendency is to consistently follow through. Choose to be consistent. As a Sanguine-Melancholy you may struggle with various fears whereas the Choleric tendency is to not allow fear to stop them form achieving their goal. Choose to overcome your fears. Adding these two tendencies to your behavior will make you a more effective person.

    ☐ I choose to be consistent.

    ☐ I choose to overcome my fears.

Questions For Reflection and Growth

1. Select one that needs the most attention now and what will you do?

_____

_____

_____

2. Write down the problems that have occurred because of a lack of these tendencies in your daily behavior. Be specific and brief.

_____

_____

_____

3. Now write out the reasons why you should practice these tendencies. How will it help you to become a more balanced person? Be specific and brief.

_____

_____

_____

4. Write out how you will incorporate these characteristics into your daily behavior. Be specific and brief.

_____

_____

_____

Sanguine-Melancholy Needs

Select 10 of the following temperament needs:

CHECK ✓ ONLY 10

1. ☐ I need a plan.
2. ☐ I need to have fun.
3. ☐ I need to be led gently, don't push on me.
4. ☐ I need feedback.
5. ☐ I need brief and direct answers.

6. ☐ I need to know the big picture.
7. ☐ I need to know I'm appreciated.
8. ☐ I need freedom from details.
9. ☐ I need low key correction.
10. ☐ I need to tell people what to do.

11. ☐ I need time to think.
12. ☐ I need to learn by doing.
13. ☐ I need to have frequent talks.
14. ☐ I need to be by myself when bothered.
15. ☐ I need social involvement with my friends.

16. ☐ I need tolerance when I get aggressive.
17. ☐ I need to know why.
18. ☐ I need you to *show* me first then *tell* me how.
19. ☐ I need the freedom to talk.
20. ☐ I need to ask questions.

21. ☐ I need a stable environment.
22. ☐ I need you to not hang over my shoulder.
23. ☐ I need help so I will not seek perfection.
24. ☐ I need facts logically given.
25. ☐ I need you to get to the point.

26. ☐ I need help organizing.
27. ☐ I need to say it only once.
28. ☐ I need to talk about what's bothering me.
29. ☐ I need time to adjust to change.
30. ☐ I need to know the results expected.

31. ☐ I need to know exactly what is expected of me.
32. ☐ I need reassurance that I'm doing the job right.
33. ☐ I need a flexible schedule.
34. ☐ I need information.
35. ☐ I need help handling rejection.

36. ☐ I need you to help me say "no."
37. ☐ I need you to tell me only once.
38. ☐ I need you to help me do things *right*.
39. ☐ I need social activity.
40. ☐ I need you to help me get results quickly.

Write down the ten needs you selected and their number **in order of their importance**. Which one is the most important, which one is the next important, etc. Also, rate how well each need is being met on a scale of one to ten.

For example: #17   I need to know why.

How well is this need being met?   10—9—⑧—7—6—5—4—3—2—1

1. #_____   _____

How well is this need being met?   10—9—8—7—6—5—4—3—2—1

2. #_____   _____

How well is this need being met?   10—9—8—7—6—5—4—3—2—1

3. #_____   _____

How well is this need being met?   10—9—8—7—6—5—4—3—2—1

4. #_____   _____

How well is this need being met?   10—9—8—7—6—5—4—3—2—1

5. #_____   _____

How well is this need being met?   10—9—8—7—6—5—4—3—2—1

6. #_____   _____

How well is this need being met?   10—9—8—7—6—5—4—3—2—1

7. #_____   _____

How well is this need being met?   10—9—8—7—6—5—4—3—2—1

8. #_____   _____

How well is this need being met?   10—9—8—7—6—5—4—3—2—1

9. #_____   _____

How well is this need being met?   10—9—8—7—6—5—4—3—2—1

10. #_____   _____

How well is this need being met?   10—9—8—7—6—5—4—3—2—1

Questions For Reflection and Growth

Answer the following questions:

Is your most important need being met? ☐ Yes ☐ No

If "No," complete the following:

Write out how you will incorporate this need into your daily behavior. Be specific and brief.

_____

_____

Which needs are not being met? What can you change to meet these needs?

_____

_____

_____

_____

_____

_____

_____

_____

How can you lovingly share those needs with those who are important to you?

_____

_____

Sanguine-Melancholy
Responses Needed From Others

You prefer other people to respond to you a certain way. Check ✓ all that you would like others to do for you:

☐ I would like others to understand that I need to be with people
most of the time but *not all the time*.

      Needed 10—9—8—7—6—5—4—3—2—1 Not needed

☐ I would like others to understand that I need alone time every day.

      Needed 10—9—8—7—6—5—4—3—2—1 Not needed

☐ I would like others to understand I like to have a plan.

      Needed 10—9—8—7—6—5—4—3—2—1 Not needed

☐ I would like others to understand that I need a reason to change my plans.

      Needed 10—9—8—7—6—5—4—3—2—1 Not needed

☐ I would like others to not embarrass me especially in public.

      Needed 10—9—8—7—6—5—4—3—2—1 Not needed

☐ I would like others to give me the big picture so I will know what to expect.

      Needed 10—9—8—7—6—5—4—3—2—1 Not needed

Be careful with whom (and how) you share these request. It's meant to be shared with family and friends, and if you hold a position of authority, those under your supervision. Don't demand that others do theses things, just explain that this is your preferred way to be treated and you will do the same for them. This will help you develop patience. See the next page for *effective responses* and follow these rules:

**If I meet the needs of your temperament it will increase
the possibility of a favorable response.**

**The way people communicate with you
is the way they want you to communicate with them.**

The Sanguine-Melancholy's Environment Needed

As a Sanguine-Melancholy you function best in an environment that meets your temperament needs. Make careful, responsible choices, that provide the best environment for you to flourish and be at your best.

Check ✓ all of those that represent a preferred environment and rate each on a scale of one to ten:

☐ Opportunity to be creative   Needed 10—9—8—7—6—5—4—3—2—1 Not needed
☐ A variety of activities   Needed 10—9—8—7—6—5—4—3—2—1 Not needed
☐ Acceptance   Needed 10—9—8—7—6—5—4—3—2—1 Not needed
☐ Recognition for accomplishments   Needed 10—9—8—7—6—5—4—3—2—1 Not needed
☐ Opportunity to plan   Needed 10—9—8—7—6—5—4—3—2—1 Not needed
☐ Rules that are reasonable   Needed 10—9—8—7—6—5—4—3—2—1 Not needed
☐ Opportunity to build relationships   Needed 10—9—8—7—6—5—4—3—2—1 Not needed
☐ Private time   Needed 10—9—8—7—6—5—4—3—2—1 Not needed

1. Are you in an environment that best fits your temperament needs?   ☐ Yes ☐ No

2. What can you do to improve your environment?

_____

_____

_____

_____

_____

Effective Responses

For the Choleric:

•Be brief, to the point.

•Be direct.

•Be confident.

•Give them facts.

•Be result oriented.

•Be practical.

•Help them save time.

•Be objective, matter-of-fact.

•Discuss getting better, faster results.

•Tolerate their assertive, forceful responses, and their crisis style of communication.

For the Sanguine:

•Be friendly and open.

•Build the relationship.

•Be personal.

•Be willing to listen.

•Never embarrass them.

•Spend informal time with them.

•Provide them with details.

•Remind them often, they easily forget.

•Be open about self, feelings, opinions.

•Tolerate their impulsiveness and need to talk.

For the Phlegmatic:

•Be warm and personal.

•Show interest in family.

•Use visual aids.

•Have a slow pace.

•Never hurry a conversation.

•Be in control of your emotions.

•Be willing to repeat information.

•Avoid asking for sudden change.

•Tell them you "sincerely" appreciate efforts.

•Tolerate their slow pace and lack of a sense of urgency.

For the Melancholy:

•Be considerate and personal.

•Allow time for research.

•Give reassurance.

•Give feedback.

•Give lots of information.

•Listen carefully to their ideas.

•Be specific, factual and logical.

•Discuss what is "right" or "best."

•Give specific, detailed, instructions.

•Tolerate their need to check for accuracy and time to think about a proposal.

If you are **angry**

you're living in the past.

If you are **anxious**

you're living in the future.

If you are **depressed** you're

thinking about the wrong thing.

If you have **peace**

you're living in the present

and trusting God.

PART III

Biblical Principles To Practice For Spiritual Growth

If you are **angry**

you're living in the past.

If you are **anxious**

you're living in the future.

If you are **depressed** you're

thinking about the wrong thing.

If you have **peace**

you're living in the present

and trusting God.

Chapter 6

Introduction to Living the Spiritual Life

Why this section? Every Christian, regardless of their temperament blend, struggles with the issues that will be discussed. Disobedience isn't reserved to a specific temperament. All Christians have the same problem, we disobey God. For example, the four temperaments all have an issue with anger, but for different reasons. The Choleric will likely show anger because a goal was not accomplished, a Sanguine may show anger if they are embarrassed in public, the Phlegmatic may show anger if their routine is interrupted, and the Melancholy may show anger if they think an injustice has been done. So, all Christians need to work on not being angry regardless of the reason.

Of course, living the spiritual life is not easy. It is a process of growth that last a *life* time. To live as God wants us to requires unlearning patterns of thinking, feeling, and behaving that do not represent what the Bible teaches. We have to replace those patterns of thinking and behaving with how God says we should think and behave ... and that takes time.

Learning about your natural temperament tendencies and how to use and overcome the negative impact on yourself and others is a start. Next, practice the following Biblical principles daily:

1. The Purpose of The Christian Life
2. Trust God No Matter What
3. Renovate Your Thinking
4. How To Develop Self-Control
5. How To Deal With Frustration
6. Do Not Be Anxious.
7. Do Not Get Angry
8. Do Not Argue
9. Two Kinds of Guilt
10. The Cause and Cure of Depression
11. How Love Behaves
12. How to Treat People

The Scripture is very clear. It is not enough to **know** what God has said, you have to **do** what God has said. James 1:22 *But be **doers** of the word, and not hearers only, **deceiving** yourselves.*

What's the deception? The deception is believing that just knowing is enough! But God wants you to be a **doer**. The Greek word for *doer* means to be a *performer*, so you are to *perform* His Word. Also, the word *doer* is in the present tense which means you are to *continually* do His Word.

The Greek word for *deceive* means you are guilty of *false reasoning*. So if you know the Word and do not do the Word you have *reasoned incorrectly*. God wants you to put the Word into practice and *perform* it in your life daily.

The process for this to happen is to first become *aware* of what you need to do, then *accept ownership* of what you need to do, and then actually *change your thinking and behavior* to *do* what God says.

Overcomers Will be Rewarded

To grow spiritually you must decide to use *self-control* to overcome sin as discussed throughout Scripture. This is not an easy process nor does it happen quickly. If you overcome you will live a life that is pleasing to the Lord. Remember that God will always be there to help you; Psalm 23 and Philippians 4:13. You not only will be *transformed* into Christ likeness but you will be rewarded for a life well lived. The following is from my brother Mike's book *How God Treats People*:

> According to 1 John 5:4 all believers are *overcomers*, but the present tense in the very next verse (1 Jn. 5:5) indicates that believers who continue are *overcomers*. In the book of Revelation, faithful believers are *overcomers* (Rev. 2:26).
>
> The point of the Lord telling the seven churches of Revelation about the *overcomer* getting a reward is to motivate them to live in such a way as they will receive the reward at the Judgment Seat of Christ. Do not be overcome; become an *overcomer*. In short, the *overcomer* is the believer who is rewarded for being a spiritual victor over circumstances in this life and not a victim of them.
>
> What must believers do to receive an additional inheritance? The meek shall inherit the earth (Mt. 5:5), that is, the meek, "those who do not demand their own rights, will have a special place of rule in the kingdom" (Wall, p. 83). The righteous, who help the needy, will inherit the kingdom (Mt. 25:34). Believers who are rich in faith are heirs of the kingdom (Jas. 2:5). Those who bless others will inherit a blessing (1 Pet. 3:9). Believers who suffer for Christ will be a joint-heir with Christ (Rom. 8:17). Those who heed what they have heard (Heb. 2:1) will inherit "eschatological salvation" (Heb. 1:14). Those who have faith and patience inherit the promises (Heb. 6:12, 14). The *overcomer* will inherit all things (Rev. 21:7).

Think Biblically

James 1:22 *But be **doers** of the word, and not hearers only, **deceiving** yourselves.*

The rest of this section has Biblical principles that will help you grow spiritually ... if you apply them to your life daily. Remember, obeying what God has said will result in you being transformed into the *likeness of Christ* and you will receive an award as an *overcomer*.

1. The Purpose of The Christian Life

Romans 8:28-29

28 And we know that all things work together for good to those who love God, to those who are the called according to His purpose. 29 For whom He foreknew, He also pre-destined to be conformed to the image of His Son, that He might be the firstborn among many brethren.

For the Christian, there are two ways to look at what happens in your life. You are either a *victim* of your circumstances or there is divine *purpose* involved.

God's divine purpose for life's events is identified in Romans 8:28-29. The passage states that *all things work together for good*. It does not say some, many, or most things work together, but *all* things. The accident, the lost relationship, the failed marriage, the rebellious child, the lost job, illness, financial crisis, scratching your favorite shoes, the fire, being betrayed by a family member or friend, failing to accomplish a goal, etc. I cannot possible mentioned everything someone may go through in life but you get the idea. All things, yes everything, that happens in your life *can be used* by God to conform you into the image of His Son, no exceptions! This means that...

God doesn't do anything TO you, He does it FOR you.

This is why you are not a victim of your circumstances. God will use *anything* and *everything* to help conform you into the image of His Son!

Now notice, the passage does not say that *all things are good* or that God *causes all things*. It says that *all things* are being **used for good**. The Greek word for *good* includes in the definition the idea of *benefit*. So all the events in your life have **benefit** in conforming you into the image of His Son. Of course, you may not see the *benefit* when the event occurs but have faith that God will somehow use the events and people to accomplish the goal of conforming you into a likeness of His Son.

This is what it means to walk by faith; you may not see how the event will be *beneficial* but God does. Trust God that He knows what He is doing in your past, current, and future circumstances.

The former coach of the Dallas Cowboys Tom Landry (1924-2000) was reported to have said, "We learn out of our failures not out of our successes." Imagine if your life went smoothly and you were able to get everything you wanted when you wanted it, and you had plenty of money, you never got sick, and your family and friends prospered. Would you need God for anything? The ups and downs of life are designed to get your attention so you will let God conform you into His image.

Think Biblically

Everything that happens in my life is used by God to help me
become conformed into the image of Jesus Christ.

2. Trust God No Matter What

Proverbs 3:5-6

Trust in the Lord with all your heart, And lean not on your own understanding;
6 In all your ways acknowledge Him, And He shall direct your paths.

That's right, God wants you to trust Him no matter what is happening in your life. Notice the contrast in verse 6 is between **trusting the Lord** and **trusting *your* understanding**. If we trust the Lord, we cannot *also* depend upon our reasoning to understand what God is doing. Many times we cannot make sense out of it.

Sumner Wemp, my spiritual grandfather, said to me, that Proverbs 3:5-6 is teaching us "Don't try to figure it out."

Just trust that the Lord knows what He is doing. Do not forget that it is God Who is directing your life. It is God Who determines what is best for you. It is God Who has the final decision. Not you, it is God Who sees the whole picture while we see only a tiny piece. Someone put it this way;

> To trust in the Lord with all our heart means we can't place our own right to understand above His right to direct our lives the way He sees fit. When we insist on God always making sense to our finite minds, we are setting ourselves up for spiritual trouble.

My brother, Mike, made this comment on Proverbs 3:5-6:

> The Hebrew word for "direct" means "smooth, straight, right." Smooth is being free from obstacles. These verses are not promising daily direction in all the decisions we make. They are saying that if we follow the Lord, He will make our lives go straight in the sense of righteousness, smooth in the sense of removing all hindrances out of the way.

Our limited understanding can easily lead us down the wrong path. Just trust that the Lord knows what He is doing in your life.

Joshua 1:9 *Have I not commanded you? Be strong and of good courage; do not be afraid, nor be dismayed, for the Lord your God is with you wherever you go.*

Isaiah 41:10 *Fear not, for I am with you; Be not dismayed, for I am your God. I will strengthen you, Yes, I will help you, I will uphold you with My righteous right hand.*

Matthew 6:26-27 *Look at the birds of the air; they do not sow or reap or store away in barns, and yet your heavenly Father feeds them. Are you not much more valuable than they? Can any one of you by worrying add a single hour to your life?*

John 14:1 *Do not let your hearts be troubled. You believe in God; believe also in Me.*

Psalm 27:14 *Wait on the Lord; Be of good courage, And He shall strengthen your heart; Wait, I say, on the Lord*!

Think Biblically

Make this a part of what you think:

I will trust God no matter what happens in my life.

Remember:

God doesn't do anything **TO** me, He does it **FOR** me.

3. Renovate Your Thinking

Romans 12:1-2

I beseech you therefore, brethren, by the mercies of God, that you present your bodies a living sacrifice, holy, acceptable to God, which is your reasonable service. 2 And do not be conformed to this world, but be transformed by the renewing of your mind, that you may prove what is that good and acceptable and perfect will of God.

This passage teaches that in order for change to occur in your behavior you have to change what you have been thinking. To understand the flow of this passage I've isolated the main thoughts in verses 1 and 2 as follows:

I beseech you therefore, brethren, by the mercies of God, that you present your bodies a living sacrifice, holy, acceptable to God, which is your reasonable service.

Romans chapter 12:1 marks a turning point in the epistle. Paul uses the term *therefore* which means he has made a point in previous chapters and now he is going to apply what he has said. For example, Paul has said that because we have been *justified by faith, we have peace with God* (5:1). *I beseech you therefore* ... Paul strongly encourages (beseech is not a command) us to give ourselves as a *living sacrifice* to Him. It's only *reasonable*, the Greek word means *logical*, *s*o, it's *logical* for us to give back to Him *ourselves* as a *living sacrifice*. How then do we do that?

do not be conformed to his world

First, in verse 2 Paul instructs us to *not be conformed to this world.* The word *conformed* means simply *to be like.* There are two words in the Greek New Testament translated *world.* One is *cosmos* which means *universe.* The other word is *aion* which means *age.* The word used in verse 2 is *aion.* So Paul is saying that we are not *to be like* the *age* in which we live.

but be transformed

You are to be *transformed by the renewing of your mind.* Transformation is the process we are to go through in order to change. The word *transformation* appears only twice in the New Testament; Romans 12:2 and 2 Corinthians 3:18. You will recognize the Greek word translated "transform" is *metamorphoo* from which we get the word *metamorphosis.* According to Strong's Hebrew and Greek Dictionary, this Greek word means *to change to a different pattern, to change into a wholly different form or appearance.*

God has given us an example of *transformation* in nature. Every butterfly begins life as a caterpillar, goes through a *transformation,* and becomes a completely different life form. This is what every believer is to experience in their spiritual growth. It will happen when you practice daily doing what God has said.

I need to get technical to communicate an important truth. The Greek word for *transformation* (*metamorphoo*) is a verb that is in the present, passive, imperative form. All that means this: *present* means this is an ongoing action. The *passive imperative* is a command directed to you in which you are *not* the active doer, but rather the *cooperator* and *recipient* of someone else's doing, and yet you still retain responsibility.

So, *transformation* (change) happens **to** you. You *do not* do the changing, you *receive* the change. You are continually responsible to *do* something (mentioned next) and then change will occur. What are you supposed to do continually?

by the renewing of your mind

The meaning of the word *renew* holds the secret as to what anyone must do to change. The word *renew* means to **renovate**. Now what happens when you renovate something? You take out the *old* and put in the *new*!

> Remodeling a house illustrates renovation. A designer and contractor will take a used, often old home, and make it look brand new. To achieve the makeover they will take out the old fixtures, and sometimes walls, and replace the old fixtures with new ones. When finished it's impossible to see the condition it was once in.

The same process is necessary for you to change. According to *Thayer's Greek-English Lexicon of The New Testament*, the meaning of the Greek word for *mind* (*nous*) includes thoughts, feelings, purposes, and desires. So what needs to change is the way you are dealing with people and life situations.

Common issues include; anxiety, fear, frustration, irritation, anger, arguing, depression, guilt, lack of forgiveness, addictions, etc. Here's the idea. If you do any of these things it's because you *think it's okay*. To be transformed you must choose to think that these things **are not okay**.

Think Biblically: Do it God's way. Change the way you have been thinking and practice the things that are discussed in this workbook.

4. How To Develop Self-Control

Self-control is a virtue that reflects spiritual growth and maturity. It's so important that (as mentioned) every book in the New Testament has instructions to *put on, put off, start, stop*. All the writers encouraged Christians to *stop* bad behavior and *start* Godly behavior.

1. The Greek word for *self-control* (translated *temperance*) as found in Galatians 5:23, 2 Pet. 1:6, and Titus 1:8 is defined (by Thayer's Greek Definitions) "as one who masters his desires and passions, especially his sensual appetites, mastering, controlling, curbing, restraining, controlling one's self, temperate, continent."

What is it about *self* that needs controlling? You need to control what you *think*, what you *feel*, what you *do,* and what you *say*.

To achieve self-control you need to change your thinking to align with what God wants you think, feel, do, and say. Note the following passages:

Control your thoughts. 1 Peter. 1:13 Peter says, *Therefore gird up the loins of your mind, be sober, and rest your hope fully upon the grace that is to be brought to you at the revelation of Jesus Christ.* The word "self-control" does not appear in this passage but the idea is clearly there. The way to control the mind is by thinking about something else. Paul says in Philippians. 4:8 *Finally, brethren, whatever things are true, whatever things are noble, whatever things are just, whatever things are pure, whatever things are lovely, whatever things are of good report, if there is any virtue and if there is anything praiseworthy — meditate on these things.*

Control your emotions. Ephesians. 4:31-32 *Let all bitterness, wrath, anger, clamor, and evil speaking be put away from you, with all malice. And be kind to one another, tenderhearted, forgiving one another, just as God in Christ forgave you.* Again, the word self-control does not appear, but the concept is present.

Control your behavior. Proverbs 4:23-27 *Keep* [guard] *your heart with all diligence, For out of it spring the issues* [boundaries] *of life. Guard what you say. 24 Put away from you a deceitful mouth, And put perverse lips far from you. Guard what you say. 25 Let your eyes look straight ahead, And your eyelids look right before you. Guard where you go. 26 Ponder the path of your feet, And let all your ways be established. 27 Do not turn to the right or the left; Remove your foot from evil.*

Control your speech. Ephesians 4: 29 *Let no corrupt word proceed out of your mouth, but what is good for necessary edification, that it may impart grace to the hearers.*

Control your sexual desires. 1 Corinthians 6:18-20 *Flee sexual immorality. Every sin that a man does is outside the body, but he who commits sexual immorality sins against his own body. 19 Or do you not know that your body is the temple of the Holy Spirit who is in you, whom you have from God, and you are not your own? 20 For you were bought at a price; therefore glorify God in your body and in your spirit, which are God's.*

2. To develop self-control requires the following:

   Impulse control: The choice to resist the urge to engage in behaviors that are impulsive or rewarding at the moment.

   Delayed gratification: The choice to wait for a more valuable reward in the future rather than opting for an immediate, lesser reward.

   Emotional regulation: The choice to maintain composure under stress and not react with extreme emotions.

   Cognitive control: The choice to control your thoughts to stay focused on tasks, resist distractions, and manage stress or frustration.

   Behavioral inhibition: The choice to not engage in undesirable behaviors.

Each temperament blend has its own challenges and struggles that differ from the other temperament blends. Your challenges to gaining self-control are, in part, related to the weaknesses mentioned earlier in this workbook. Regardless of one's temperament we are all required to gain self-control.

3. What does the Bible say about one who does not have self-control?

   Proverbs 16:32 *Better a patient person than a warrior, those with self-control than those who take a city.*

   Proverbs 25:28 *Like a city whose walls are broken through is a person who lacks self-control.*

   James 1:6-8 in part states ... *he is a double-minded man, unstable in all his ways.*

Lacking self-control leads to instability, vulnerability, and being unstable in all your ways. One who lacks self-control cannot grow to spiritual maturity.

4. What does the Bible say about one who has self-control? Self-control produces contentment. Cultivating self-control is essential for spiritual growth, maturity, wisdom, discipline, and living a Godly life.

   Philippians 4:11-13 *Not that I speak in regard to need, for I have learned in whatever state I am, to be content: 12 I know how to be abased, and I know how to abound. Everywhere and in all things I have learned both to be full and to be hungry, both to abound and to suffer need. 13 I can do all things through Christ who strengthens me.*

   Hebrews 13:5-6 *5 Let your conduct be without covetousness; be content with such things as you have. For He Himself has said, "I will never leave you nor forsake you." 6 So we may boldly say: "The Lord is my helper; I will not fear. What can man do to me?"*

5. What does it mean to be content? Being content means that when life doesn't turn out like you thought it would you accept it as coming from God for your benefit. It means that you do not get anxious or angry. It means you live a peaceful life free from overreacting to setbacks.

Being content does not mean you should become passive and disengage living life. The Apostle Paul was content but he still had goals, plans, and ambitions.

> **Romans 15:22-24** *For this reason I also have been much hindered from coming to you. 23 But now no longer having a place in these parts, and having a great desire these many years to come to you, 24 whenever I journey to Spain, I shall come to you. For I hope to see you on my journey, and to be helped on my way there by you, if first I may enjoy your company for a while. 25 But now I am going to Jerusalem to minister to the saints.*

6. Believers are to exercise self-control in every area of life. Paul says in **I Corinthians 9:25** *And everyone who competes for the prize is temperate (self-control) in all things. Now they do it to obtain a perishable crown, but we for an imperishable crown.*

PART III "Biblical Principles To Practice For Spiritual Growth" include things for you to practice in order to develop self-control. I know, it's not going to be easy, but it is necessary to grow spiritually. Pick an issue from the list shown below and follow the four steps suggested below.

Trust God No Matter What
Self-Control
How To Deal With Frustration
Do Not Be Anxious.
Do Not Get Angry
Do Not Argue
The Cause and Cure of Depression
How Love Behaves
How to Treat People

7. Four steps to follow to gain self-control. You can use the steps for any issue with witch you are struggling but to illustrate let's use dealing with anger.

A. **Accept responsibility:**
Before you can move toward to a better way of living you must accept responsibility for the choices that you have made. From those choices you developed patterns of thinking, feeling, and behaving that are causing the issue with which you are now struggling.

☐ I struggle with getting angry.

B: **Make the decision to stop:**

Change starts with a decision. You must decide that you want too reverse and overcome the unhealthy patterns you have developed. This sounds simple, or even easy, but it's actually the hardest part! Every person that has changed their behavior first accepted responsibility for what they were doing and decided to change.

☐ I decide to stop getting angry.

C. **Ask God to help you:**

As a Christian, you are not expected to fight the battle by yourself. God wants you call on Him for help. Here are two passages to depend on for God's help.

Hebrews 4:16 *Let us therefore come boldly to the throne of grace, that we may obtain mercy and find grace to help in time of need.*

Proverbs 3:5-7 *Trust in the Lord with all your heart, And lean not on your own understanding; 6 In all your ways acknowledge Him, And He shall direct your paths. 7 Do not be wise in your own eyes; Fear the Lord and depart from evil.*

☐ I ask God to help me to stop getting angry.

D. **Do this every time you get angry:**

As soon as you realize you're angry, stop, ask God to forgive you. Quote this verse **Ephesians 4:31-32** *Let all bitterness, wrath, anger, clamor, and evil speaking be put away from you, with all malice. 32 And be kind to one another, tenderhearted, forgiving one another, even as God in Christ forgave you.*

☐ I will ask for God's forgiveness and stop being angry.

If every time to get angry, and stop, you will eventually be *transformed* according to Romans 12:2 (see pages 53-54). When you are transformed by the work of the Holy Spirit you will no longer want to get angry! It will take time so don't give up.

Repeat these steps for any issue with which you are struggling and you will be transformed and content.

5. How To Deal With Frustration

Frustration can be defined as an *anticipated goal or desire that is left unsatisfied*. It is a feeling of disappointment or exasperation. Of course, everyone has experienced *frustration* during their life.

Simply put, frustration comes from **expectations not met**. We expect people to perform and events to occur. Admittedly, sometimes our expectations are unrealistic or we place too much importance on our expectations.

Expectations not met may cause a series of reactions to occur if each stage is not redirected:

Frustration → Anger → Bitterness → Depression

If your depression is not dealt with it could lead to one or more irrational acts:

☐ Revenge   ☐ Withdrawal   ☐ Irritability

☐ Weeping   ☐ Critical attitude   ☐ Aggression

What is the solution? **Turn the page →**

ADJUST!

As soon as you recognize that you are frustrated (and it may not be immediately obvious to you) say **ADJUST!** to yourself. This will stop the chain of bad feelings from unfolding as mentioned on the previous page. Now think about doing one of the following to end the feeling of frustration:

1. **I choose not to be frustrated.**

    ☐ Everything is a choice.

2. **I will choose another way of looking at what just happened** (I will change my perception).

    ☐ It's not what happened that frustrates me, it's what I think about what happened.

    ☐ How can I look at this so it's not a problem?

    ☐ I will look for a positive/different interpretation of what just happened.

3. **I choose to acknowledge what IS without making a value judgment.**

    ☐ I choose not to jump to conclusions.

    ☐ I choose to be objective and operate on facts.

4. **I choose not to take it personally.**

    ☐ God doesn't do anything to me, He does it for me.

    ☐ Romans 8:28-29   What does God want me to learn?

Now, to help you remember to **ADJUST** make a 3x5 card with **ADJUST** in big letters on one side and put the four ways to **ADJUST** on the other side.

See next page →

ADJUST! 3 X 5 Card

Fill out several 3x5 cards (as illustrated below) to have with you. For example put one in your pocket/purse, car, desk, etc. Plan to always have one available to remind you what to do. Practice ADJUSTING until you ADJUST automatically. This will take some time so don't give up, plan on ADJUSTING until you no longer get frustrated with people or events.

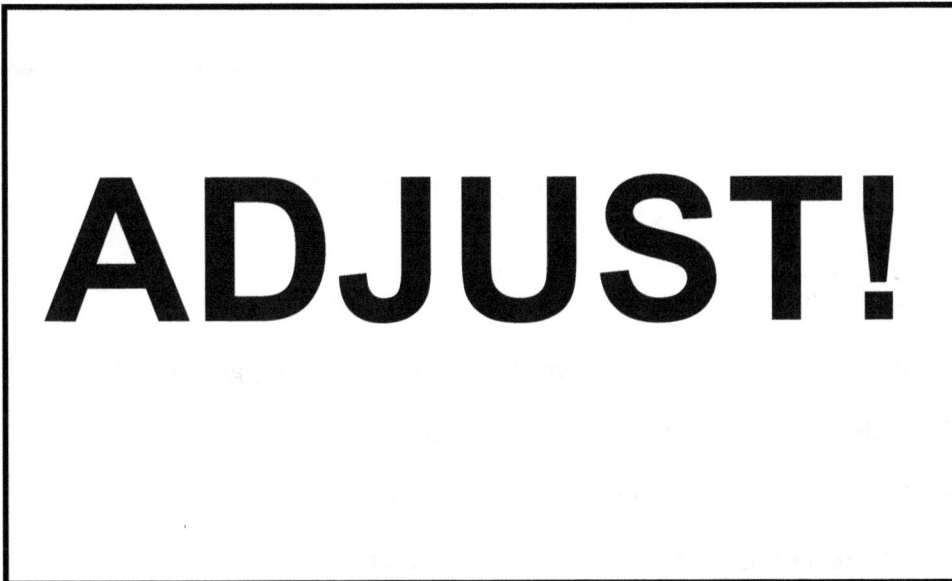

ADJUST!

1. **I choose Not to Get Frustrated**

    Everything is a choice.

2. **I will change My Perception (Reframe)**

    It's not what happens, it's what I think about what happens.
    How can I look at this so it's not a problem?
    Look for a positive/different interpretation of the event.

3. **I Acknowledge What is Without Making a Value Judgment**

    I will be objective and operate on facts.

4. **I Do Not Take it Personally**

    God doesn't do anything to me, He does it for me.
    Romans 8:28-29 What does God want me to learn?

Maturity

Maturity is directly related to how long it takes you to
respond Biblically (Adjust) to a negative event.

Disturbing Event   Biblical Response

↓   How Long Does It Take You To Adjust   ↓

?

WELL ADJUSTED PEOPLE

1. Not selfish; healthy people can get "outside" of themselves.

   Emotionally healthy people give themselves to something bigger then themselves.

2. Have the ability to have intimacy, love, and compassion.

3. Sufficiently objective about self to know both strengths and weaknesses,

   and has a planned program for overcoming the weaknesses.

4. Willing to adjust; deals with frustration, and irritations without becoming bitter or hostile.

5. Realistic perception; able to see things as they are, not as you wish them to be.

6. Sense of humor; can laugh at self.

7. Unifying philosophy of life; guided by Biblical principles not emotion.

8. Has meaning and direction.

9. Accountable for thoughts, feelings, and actions; takes ownership.

10. Willing to accept what life deals without severe emotional reaction.

If you were to apply this outline you would eventually gain complete control
over that which disturbs you. Consciously and willfully think about
ADJUSTING quickly every time you are frustrated.

The A B C's of Life

What disturbs you is not *what* happens but what the you *think* about what happens. It's not the event, it's what the you think about the event.

A. "People are disturbed, not by things or events, but by the views (perceptions) which they take of them."

Epictetus, 1st Century, A.D.

B. Since then it is my view (perception) that causes me to be disturbed ...

C. What should my view (perception) be so that I'm not disturbed?

A Biblical Perspective:

1. God does not do anything to you, He does it for you.
   Romans 8:28-29

2. How can I look at this so it's not a problem?
   James 1

3. Instead of thinking too much about the wrong thing,
   focus your thinking on how to solve the problem.
   Philippines 4

4. Answer the question, "what is God's view toward
   what is upsetting me"?
   Proverbs 3:5-6

Do this:

When you get frustrated, and it lingers for some time, it is because you are rehearsing the painful event over and over. You are focused on the problem. Instead, focus on solving the problem by asking yourself this question, **"How can I look at this so it's not a problem?"** If you focus on solving the problem you will not be thinking about the problem. Write down several ways to solve the problem.

Ephesians 4:32

And be kind to one another, tenderhearted,
forgiving one another, even as God
in Christ forgave you.

6. Do Not Be Anxious
Philippians 4:6-7

Be anxious for nothing, but in everything by prayer and supplication, with thanksgiving, let your requests be made known to God; 7 and the peace of God, which surpasses all understanding, will guard your hearts and minds through Christ Jesus.

It is a **command**, not a suggestion, to *be anxious for nothing*.

When you are feeling anxious about anything, it is because you are not trusting the Lord for the outcome of your concern; the word *anxious* means to be *troubled*.

Here is a breakdown of Philippians 4:6-7.

Do not be anxious about anything,	We are not permitted to worry about anything.
but in every situation,	No exceptions, ever.
by prayer and petition,	Prayer means "to ask"; state your exact concern.
with thanksgiving,	Now, thank God for what He is going to do. Be willing to accept the results as God's will.
present your requests to God.	Be clear, present the requests to God.
the peace of God,	You will have *calm assurance* that God is in control.
which transcends all understanding,	You will no longer be *troubled* or *anxious*.
will guard your hearts and your minds	Your thoughts and feelings will be guarded.

Guard is the greek word *garrison*. Philippi was a military town and they were there to guard (garrison) the area. If you *choose* not to be anxious and you are willing to accept what God will do about your *worry* then He will *guard* your heart. Guard your heart from what? Worry.

The word *heart* here includes mind and emotions. You will have such peace that you will not be able to understand it.

Think Biblically: Philippians 3:5 Be anxious for nothing!

Anxiety Worksheet

1. What is my **anxiety**? Write it below, be specific?

   _____

2. What is the worst that could happen if my **anxiety** is realized?

   _____

3. What is the probability of me coping if the worst happened?

   ☐ Possible   ☐ Impossible

   Why? _____

4. What are three Bible verses that tell me what to do with my **anxiety**?

   ☐ _____

   ☐ _____

   ☐ _____

5. Is my **anxiety** exaggerated?

   ☐ Yes   ☐ No

6. Have I underestimated God's ability to answer my prayer and give me peace?

   ☐ Yes   ☐ No

7. An effective way to deal with my **anxiety** is to:

   ☐ Be fearful and worry.

   ☐ Be anxious for nothing! (Philippians 3:5)

   ☐ Trust God and thank Him for whatever He does.

7. Do Not Get Angry

Ephesians 4:26

Be ye angry and sin not, let not the sun go down on your wrath.

Righteous indignation is a form of anger that is not considered sin. It is an emotional reaction over a sense of injustice like the mistreatment of another person. Jesus, for example, drove the money lenders out of the temple, Matthew 21:12-13.

All other anger is sin. Consider the following passages:

Proverbs 15:1 *A gentle answer turns away wrath, but a harsh word stirs up anger.*

Proverbs 15:18 *A hot-tempered person stirs up conflict, but the one who is patient calms a quarrel.*

Proverbs 19:19 *A man of great wrath will suffer punishment; For if you rescue him, you will have to do it again.*

Ecclesiastes 7:9 *Do not be quickly provoked in your spirit, for anger resides in the lap of fools.*

I Corinthians 13:5 *Love is not provoked.*

Ecclesiastes 7:9 *Do not hasten in your spirit to be angry, For anger rests in the bosom of fools.*

Believers are not allowed to get angry but if you do, God says deal with it quickly; before the sun goes down. Anger harms relationships and divides.

The Fence

There once was a young boy with a very bad temper. The boy's father wanted to teach him a lesson so he gave him a bag of nails and told him that every time he lost his temper he must hammer a nail into their wooden fence.

On the first day of this lesson the little boy had driven 37 nails into the fence. He was really mad! Over the course of the next few weeks the little boy began to control his temper so the number of nails that were hammered into the fence dramatically decreased.

Pleased, his father suggested that he now pull out one nail for each day that he could hold his temper.

Several weeks went by and the day finally came when the young boy was able to tell his father that all the nails were gone. Very gently the father took his son by the hand and led him to the fence. "You have done very well my son," he smiled, "But look at the holes in the fence. The fence will never be the same." The little boy listened carefully as his father continued to speak.

"When you say things in anger they leave permanent scars just like these. And no matter how many times you say you're sorry the wounds will still be there."

Think Biblically

Ephesians 4:26 *Be ye angry and sin not, let not the sun go down on your wrath.*

8. Do Not Argue

Proverbs 17:14

1. **Arguing damages relationships.**

A major theme of failing relationships is arguing. What the argument centers on varies from minor to major. It doesn't matter what the disagreement is over, what matters is that the issue becomes a problem. Instead of discussing a matter objectively two people engage in making, proving, or defending their point. The goal becomes winning your point instead of coming to an agreement and the relationship is damaged. Don't think that the damage is for a moment, but in fact the damage can last for years. Routine arguing leaves a residue of resentment that builds up over time and will eventually reduce the feelings you have for the other person or destroy the relationship completely.

2. **Control your emotions.**

   Proverbs 15:18 *A hot-tempered man stirs up dissension, but a patient man calms a quarrel.*

   Proverbs 17:14 *Starting a quarrel is like breaching a dam; so drop the matter before a dispute breaks out.*

   Proverbs 17:19 *He who loves a quarrel loves sin; he who builds a high gate invites destruction.*

   Proverbs 16:32 *Better to be patient than powerful; better to have self-control than to conquer a city.*

   Ephesians 4:29 *Let no corrupt communication proceed out of your mouth, but that which is good to the use of edifying, that it may minister grace unto the hearers.*

   Ephesians 4:2 *Be ye angry and sin not, let not the sun go down on your wrath.*

3. **Love doesn't argue.** I Corinthians 13: 4-8

   Love is patient: Love never takes the opportunity to avenge itself.
   Love is not provoked: Love does not get irritated.
   Love does not seek its own: Love does not trade being right for another person's feelings.
   Love is kind: Love never offends, insults or says anything unkind.

4. Keep the peace:

God places a high value on keeping the peace. When you participate in an argument you are contributing to disturbing the peace. It is Christ-like not to argue about anything.

Romans 12:18 *If it is possible, as far as it depends on you, live at peace with everyone.*

II Thessalonians 3:16 *Now may the Lord of peace himself give you peace at all times in every way. The Lord be with you all.*

Matthew 5:9 *Blessed are the peacemakers, for they shall be called sons of God.*

John 14:27 *Peace I leave with you; my peace I give to you. Not as the world gives do I give to you. Let not your hearts be troubled, neither let them be afraid.*

Hebrews 12:14 *Strive for peace with everyone, and for the holiness without which no one will see the Lord.*

I Corinthians 14:33 *For God is not a God of confusion but of peace. As in all the churches of the saints,*

I Peter 3:9-11 *Do not repay evil for evil or reviling for reviling, but on the contrary, bless, for to this you were called, that you may obtain a blessing. For "Whoever desires to love life and see good days, let him keep his tongue from evil and his lips from speaking deceit; let him turn away from evil and do good; let him seek peace and pursue it.*

The message is clear, do not argue, keep the peace.

Think Biblically:

Do not argue, remember Proverbs 17:14
*Starting a quarrel is like breaching a dam;
so drop the matter before a dispute breaks out.*

9. Two Kinds of Guilt

1. True guilt.

You have committed sin. I John 1:8-10

> *If we claim to be without sin, we deceive ourselves and the truth is not in us. If we confess our sins, he is faithful and just and will forgive us our sins and purify us from all unrighteousness. If we claim we have not sinned, we make him out to be a liar and his word is not in us.*

2. False guilt.

You have confessed your sin to the Lord but you still feel guilty. When guilty feelings arise over sins already confessed, reject such feelings as <u>false guilt</u>.

God has forgiven you. Read and meditate on Psalm 103:8-12.

> *The LORD is compassionate and gracious, slow to anger, abounding in love. He will not always accuse, nor will he harbor his anger forever; he does not treat us as our sins deserve or repay us according to our iniquities. For as high as the heavens are above the earth, so great is his love for those who fear him; **as far as the east is from the west, so far has he removed our transgressions from us**.*

3. When guilt feelings linger.

When guilt feelings linger after confessing the sin consider these two options:

A. You may need to go to the person that you sinned against and ask forgiveness and make restitution. For example, if you stole something you should return it to the owner.

B. If guilt feelings linger and there is no one to go to then it is pride. Pride keeps the focus on "you" and what "you" have done. The focus should be on "Him" and what "He" has done. He paid the price for your sin and promised to forgive you if you confess you sin. Since He has forgiven you and has separated your sin as far as the East is from the West, what right do you have to hold on to that which has been forgiven?

Think Biblically: God does not hold onto it and neither should you!

Ephesians 4:32

And be kind to one another, tenderhearted,
forgiving one another, even as God
in Christ forgave you.

10. The Cause and Cure of Depression

Proverbs 12:25

Anxiety in the heart of man causes depression,
But a good word makes it glad.

There are only two reasons that a person gets depressed.

1. A chemical imbalance in your brain.

    There is no scientific evidence that a chemical imbalance in the brain exists that causes depression. It's only a theory. See my book *Man's Wisdom or God's Wisdom* for a treatment of the chemical imbalance theory; available online at Amazon and Barnes and Noble.

    Note: *Postpartum depression* often suffered by a mother after childbirth, is typically due to hormonal changes, psychological adjustment to motherhood, and fatigue.

2. You are *thinking too much about the wrong thing.*

    Some Christians respond to their unpleasant circumstances by becoming depressed. Depression is a feeling of sadness and dejection that alters a person's emotional and mental state and interferes with their daily life functions in varying degrees. Symptoms range from mild to severe and can be short-term or last for an extended period.

    Before I go further please understand that some down feelings are not only appropriate but normal. For example, if you were to lose a loved one to death it would be expected to feel deeply sad emotions and have normal activities like eating, sleeping, and working interrupted. After some time has elapsed these functions return to normal and we continue our journey through this life.

    For the most part, however, those who report they are "depressed" are focused on one or more problems. Life has overwhelmed them, a tragic event has happen, or something did not happened as expected, someone did something to them, or they did something to someone else ... the list is endless.
    It is different however when a Christian *routinely* gets depressed over the painful events in their life. It is different when the Christian retreats and withdraws from life to pout or fume about their circumstances. It is different when a Christian reacts negatively to events, gets angry, and depressed.
    When depression is a routine response to life's circumstances people are living examples of what Epictetus said 2,000 years ago (as mentioned earlier). Epictetus said that it is not *what* happened to you that is disturbing, it is what you *think about* what happened that is disturbing you.

Depressed people disturb themselves by holding on to their negative perception of the event. If you are depressed you are not trying to solve the problem, you are embedded in the problem by reviewing the negatives and fuming over the wrongness of the event. If you are routinely depressed you are choosing to be miserable.

If you often react this way it is because you fail to see that God is working through your circumstances to conform you into the image of His Son (Romans 8:28-29). Instead of seeing God in the situation you are viewing your circumstance as not fair, wrong, or even punishment from God. The unfairness or wrongness is what is being reviewed and rehearsed in your thoughts. All you can see is the pain and suffering you are going through and you want it to stop ... now! You are stuck in, and focused on, the problem. You fail to see or do not accept what God is doing in your life through your circumstances.

Depression and Scripture

The Bible was written over a sixteen-hundred-year period and from the beginning God had something to say about being depressed.

> **Deuteronomy 31:8** It is the LORD who goes before you. He will be with you; he will not leave you or forsake you. Do not fear or be dismayed.

> > The Hebrew word translated *leave* has the idea of *leave alone*. The word that immediately follows is *forsake* which means to *leave destitute or fail*. The Hebrew word translated *dismayed* means to *break down, either (literally) by violence, or (figuratively) by confusion and fear; to beat down, caused to be discourage.*

So Moses, the writer of Deuteronomy, has given us three reasons to not be discouraged or depressed. First, God goes before you which means He holds the future and He is leading you. Second, He is with you which means He is beside you. Thirdly, He will never fail you or leave you destitute.

With promises like this, there is no reason to ever be discouraged or depressed. God is there for you and always will be. God continued to encourage us throughout the Bible to wait on Him, to hope in Him, and to humble ourselves before Him as noted in the following verses:

> **Psalms 40:1-3** *I waited patiently for the LORD; he inclined to me and heard my cry. He drew me up from the pit of destruction, out of the miry bog, and set my feet upon a rock, making my steps secure. He put a new song in my mouth, a song of praise to our God. Many will see and fear, and put their trust in the LORD.*

> **1 Peter 5:6-7** *Humble yourselves therefore under the mighty hand of God, that he may exalt you in due time: Casting all your care upon him; for he careth for you.*

Think Biblically: Trust God that He is working in all of your circumstances.

11. How Loves Behave

I Corinthians 13:4-8

Love suffers long and is kind; love does not envy; love does not parade itself, is not puffed up; 5 does not behave rudely, does not seek its own, is not provoked, thinks no evil; 6 does not rejoice in iniquity, but rejoices in the truth; 7 bears all things, believes all things, hopes all things, endures all things.

1. Love is PATIENT - **Love never takes the opportunity to avenge itself.**

2. Love is KIND - **Love never offends, insults or says anything unkind.**

3. Love is NOT JEALOUS - Love does not desire what another person has in an evil way.

4. Love DOES NOT BRAG - Love does not draw attention to itself.

5. Love is NOT PUFFED UP - Love does not have a superior attitude.

6. Love is NOT RUDE - **Love has good manners and makes you feel comfortable.**

7. Love SEEKS NOT ITS OWN - **Love does not trade being right for another person's feelings.**

8. Love is NOT PROVOKED - **Love does not get irritated.**

9. Love THINKS NO EVIL - Love does not keep an account of evil deeds, it forgives.

10. Love DOES NOT REJOICE OVER ANOTHER'S FAULT - Love rejoices in the truth.

11. Love COVERS SIN - **Love is able to overlook any sin.**

12. Love ALWAYS BELIEVES THE BEST - Love looks at facts, not rumors.

13. Love ALWAYS LOOKS ON THE BRIGHT SIDE - Love is never pessimistic.

14. Love SUSTAINS YOU THROUGH SUFFERING - Love remains steadfast in the face of unpleasant circumstances.

15. Love WILL NEVER RUN IN DEFEAT - Love never gives up.

A Summary of I Corinthians 13:4-8 by Dr. Tom Constable

Love does not deal with other people in a way that injures their dignity. It does not insist on having its own way, nor does it put it's own interest before the needs of others. Love is not irritable or touchy, and it ***absorbs*** offenses, insults, and inconveniences for the sake of others' welfare. It does not keep a record of offenses received to pay them back.

Think Biblically: Love others.

12. How To Treat People

How you treat others is a reflection of your spiritual maturity. Spiritual growth is the result of applying Biblical truth to your life. It requires, as James directs us in 1:22, to be *"doers of the Word and not hears only."*

It is necessary to know the truth of Scripture but knowing is not enough, one must *do* what the Scripture requires before growth occurs.

> Many years ago I was counseling a couple that were having difficulties in their relationship. The current issue was that the wife was angry at her husband and would not forgive him. You would have thought he was guilty of something so horrific that God Himself would have trouble forgiving him. She was that angry! Before I go further, I have been given permission to share this story.
>
> What did he do that was so unforgiving? He cleaned the house when she wasn't there! Really! Now according to the husband, the house was in need of a serious cleaning. It had been neglected, like their two young daughters, for many months. She would stay out to the early morning hours with her friends from work. To make matters worse, the husband asked his parents to help. That was the core of her problem because she was embarrassed.
>
> Nothing I said made a difference. I then asked, "Do you want God to treat you like you treat other people (implying her husband)? She quickly said No!" I shared with her the way God treats all of us and we are to do the same with other people. Here is what I said:

A. He Loves You Unconditionally

The Bible is clear about God's love. He loves you unconditionally and nothing can separate you from His love. It is because of God's love for you that brought you to salvation.

John 3:16 *For God so loved the world that He gave His One and only Son, that whoever believes in Him shall not perish but have eternal life.*

Romans 8:38-39 *For I am convinced that neither death nor life, neither angels nor demons, neither the present nor the future, nor any powers, neither height nor depth, nor anything else in all creation, will be able to separate us from the love of God that is in Christ Jesus our Lord.*

Because God has demonstrated His love toward us we are to therefore show the same kind of love to other people. God loves us without conditions. We do not have *to do* this or that, or *not do* this or that, in order for God to love us. He loves us regardless of what we do, or not do. Every time we sin He is ready to forgive and restore. Not nearly every time, but every time!

B. He Forgives You Freely

Remember, God loved you so much that He forgave you of all your sin when you became a believer. Therefore ...

Ephesians 4:32 *Be kind and compassionate to one another, forgiving each other, just as in Christ, God forgave you.*

What can anyone do to you that is greater than what you and I did to Christ? Because of your sin and my sin He went to the cross. What right do you have, or me, to not forgive someone when Jesus has forgiven us of much greater sin? There are no conditions or limits to forgiveness.

Matthew 18:21-22 *Then Peter came up and said to Him, "Lord, how often will my brother sin against me, and I forgive him? As many as seven times?" Jesus said to him, "I do not say to you seven times, but seventy times seven.*

Jesus is saying that forgiveness has no conditions or limits. Continue to forgive, again, and again, and again, keep on forgiving. That's the way God treats you.

C. He Shows You Unlimited Grace

God shows us Grace regardless of what we have done. There is an amazing truth in the story of our Lord's crucifixion and resurrection.

Mark's record of the account (14:66 -16:20) tells how Peter denied the Lord three times the night before He was crucified. When the three women arrived at the tomb three days later to anoint Jesus with spices they discovered that He was gone. An angel told them that He is risen! Then, the angel told them to go tell the disciples ... and Peter!

What a demonstration of God's Grace! Peter had denied the Lord three times before He was crucified and God The Father told the angel to tell Mary to be sure to tell **Peter**!

God showed Grace to Peter after His darkest moment. God shows that same Grace to you. Show the same Grace to others.

Think Biblically: Remember Ephesians 4:32, Show Grace to others every chance you get.

Chapter 7

How To Know If You Are Growing Spiritually

Growing spiritually means you are becoming like Christ, thinking as He thinks, behaving as He did. The evidence of spiritual growth is in the fruit of the Spirit being demonstrated in the way you live your life. This passage gives you a check list from which you can compare your behavior.

> **Galatians 5:22-23** *But the fruit of the Spirit is love, joy, peace, longsuffering, kindness, goodness, faithfulness, gentleness, self-control. Against such there is no law.*

1. **Love** - The Greek word for love in this passage is *agape* which is self-sacrificing affection for others.

   ☐ Love people according to I Corinthians 13:5-8 (pages 75-76).

2. **Joy** - Means *calm delight* which is deep-seated gladness regardless of your circumstances. Calm delight is the result of ***knowing*** that God is working in your circumstances.

   > **James 1:2** *My brethren, count it all **joy*** [have calm delight] *when you fall into various trials.*

   ☐ I will have "calm delight" when I am in a trial because I believe God is at work for my benefit.

3. **Peace** - This is an inward tranquility and serenity that comes from knowing you are trusting God for what He is doing in your life. It's inner quietness regardless of your circumstances.

   > **Col 3:15** *Let the peace of God rule in your heart.*

   ☐ I have "peace" in my heart knowing God is at work in my circumstances.

4. **Longsuffering** - Means *patience* even under provocation or in the face of trails.

   > **James 1:4** *but let endurance* (patience) *have its complete work, that you may be complete and mature, lacking nothing.*

   ☐ I will be patient with others and in trials because God is patient with me.

5. **Kindness** - Kindness in action is sweetness of disposition, gentleness in dealing with others, graciousness.

   Ephesians 2:7 *that in the ages to come He might show the exceeding riches of His grace in His kindness toward us in Christ Jesus.*

   ☐ I will be kind to others because God is kind to me.

6. **Goodness** - Constructive action reaching out to others, goodness of words and deeds.

   Galatians 6:10 *As we have therefore opportunity, let us do good unto all men, especially unto them who are of the household of faith.*

   ☐ I will be good to others because God is good to me.

7. **Faithfulness** - Means dependability, loyalty, stability, worthy of trust.

   Proverbs 28:20 *A faithful man will abound with blessings, But he who makes haste to be rich will not go unpunished.*

   ☐ I will be faithful to God because God is faithful to me.

8. **Meekness** - Strength under control. A disposition that is even-tempered, gentle, tranquil, balanced in spirit, unpretentious, and has passions under control.

   Titus 3:2 *To speak evil of no one, to avoid quarreling, to be gentle, and to show perfect courtesy toward all people.*

   ☐ I will be gentle to others because God is gentle to me.

9. **Self-control** - is mastery of one's thoughts, feelings, behavior, desires, speech, and impulses (see pages 55-58).

   Proverbs 16:32 *Better a patient person than a warrior, one with **self-control** than one who takes a city.*

   ☐ I will diligently work at controlling my thoughts, feelings, behavior, speech, desires, and impulses.

How might your temperament affect your spiritual growth? Ultimately it's a person's heart, not temperament, that determines spiritual desire and growth.

Psalm 37:4 *Delight yourself also in the Lord, And He shall give you the desires of your heart.*

Your temperament, however, can have a significant impact on how you pursue spiritual growth. Every temperament blend must challenge and overcome some of their natural tendencies to grow spiritually.

Challenges

Shallow pursuits: Sanguines are often drawn to external pleasures, like socializing, entertainment, or material pursuits. This will distract you from introspection and meditation on Scripture fundamental to spiritual growth. If you prioritize instant gratification over reflection, it will prevent deeper understanding or alignment with spiritual goals.

Impatience: Your natural enthusiasm and desire for novelty may lead to impatience. Spiritual growth requires patience, persistence, and discipline. A tendency to jump from one idea or practice to another without consistency will delay spiritual progress.

Avoidance of challenges: Spiritual growth also involves confronting inner struggles. You are prone to avoid uncomfortable situations in favor of more enjoyable ones. This will hinder growth when faced with challenges that require change in behavior.

Lack of focus: You may have difficulty staying focus on things that are not exciting. If you aren't able to control your active mind, it will be harder for you to concentrate on spiritual things.

Dependence on social validation: Being highly social, you might seek validation or affirmation from others. This external focus can divert attention away from inner spiritual development, where inner peace, self-reflection, and surrender are important.

Spiritual growth involves altering your natural tendencies with disciplines that result in control of what you think, feel, say, and do.

Potential

Once committed, your enthusiasm to grow spiritually can influence others to get involved. Seek opportunities to serve others and do it as unto the Lord.

Ecclesiastes 9:10 *Whatever your hand finds to do, do it with all your might.*

Growing spiritually requires time, actually a *life* time. The Apostle Peter encouraged Christians to grow knowing it takes time.

2 Peter 3:18 *grow in the grace and knowledge of our Lord and Savior Jesus Christ.*

The word "grow" in this passage is used to depict the growth of a plant or infant both of which takes time to grow. So don't be hard on yourself if you are not making the progress you expected. Do not give up. Keep working on practicing the fruit of the Spirit, loving others, and doing the other things in this workbook. Remember, it takes time to be transformed.

Dr. Henry Brandt

A mature man is one who is sufficiently objective about himself
to know both his strengths and his weaknesses and to create
a planned program for overcoming his weaknesses.

Think Biblically

Recommend Books

Cocoris, John T. *Why We Do What We Do, New Insights Into The Temperament Model of Behavior.* McKinney, Texas: Temperament Dynamics LLC, 2020.

_____. *Born with a Creative Temperament.* McKinney, TX: Temperament Dynamics LLC, 2014.

_____. *Seven Steps to a Better You.* McKinney, TX: Temperament Dynamics LLC, 2014.

_____. *A Parent's Guide to Helping Your Child Develop Their Natural Temperament Tendencies.* McKinney, TX: Temperament Dynamics LLC, 2016.

_____. *Trust God No Matter What.* McKinney, TX: Temperament Dynmics LLC, 2025.

_____. *Man's Wisdom or God's Wisdom, The Cause And Cure Of Mental, Emotional, And Behavior Issues.* McKinney, TX: Temperament Dynamics LLC, 2025.

_____. *Three Reasons Christians Go To Counseling.* McKinney, TX: Temperament Dynmics LLC, 2015.

_____. *Why Girls Chase Guys After A Breakup.* McKinney, TX: Temp. Dynamics, LLC, 2020.

Cocoris, G. Michael. *Spiritual Basics: Basic Biblical Truths for Living a Spiritual Life.* Santa Monica, CA: J and M Brothers Publications, 2025.

_____. *The Spiritual Life: Clarifying the Confusion.* Santa Monica, CA: J and M Brothers Publications, 2011, 2018.

_____. *Counseling Theories, A Simple Explanation And Biblical Evaluation.* Santa Monica, CA: J and M Brothers Publications, 2024.

Temperament Blend Workbooks

Cocoris, John T. *Choleric-Sanguine Workbook: The Executive Pattern, How To Develop Your Natural Tendencies And Deal With Your Strengths And Weaknesses Biblically.* McKinney, Texas: Temperament Dynamics, LLC, 2025.

_____ *Choleric-Phlegmatic Workbook: The Director Pattern, How To Develop Your Natural Tendencies And Deal With Your Strengths And Weaknesses Biblically.* McKinney, Texas: Temperament Dynamics, LLC, 2025.

_____ *Choleric-Melancholy Workbook: The Strategist Pattern, How To Develop Your Natural Tendencies And Deal With Your Strengths And Weaknesses Biblically.* McKinney, Texas: Temperament Dynamics, LLC, 2025.

_____ *Sanguine-Choleric Workbook The Negotiator Pattern, How To Develop Your Natural Tendencies And Deal With Your Strengths And Weaknesses Biblically.* McKinney, Texas: Temperament Dynamics, LLC, 2025.

_____ *Sanguine-Phlegmatic Workbook: The Relater Pattern, How To Develop Your Natural Tendencies And Deal With Your Strengths And Weaknesses Biblically.* McKinney, Texas: Temperament Dynamics, LLC, 2025.

_____ *Sanguine-Melancholy Workbook: The Performer Pattern, How To Develop Your Natural Tendencies And Deal With Your Strengths And Weaknesses Biblically.* McKinney, Texas: Temperament Dynamics, LLC, 2025.

_____. *Phlegmatic-Choleric Workbook: The Inspector Pattern, How To Develop Your Natural Tendencies And Deal With Your Strengths And Weaknesses Biblically.* McKinney, Texas: Temperament Dynamics, LLC, 2025.

_____. *Phlegmatic-Sanguine Workbook: The Harmonizer Pattern, How To Develop Your Natural Tendencies And Deal With Your Strengths And Weaknesses Biblically.* McKinney, Texas: Temperament Dynamics, LLC, 2025.

_____. *Phlegmatic-Melancholy Workbook: Helper Pattern, How To Develop Your Natural Tendencies And Deal With Your Strengths And Weaknesses Biblically.* McKinney, Texas: Temperament Dynamics, LLC, 2025.

_____. *Melancholy-Choleric Workbook: The Instructor Pattern, How To Develop Your Natural Tendencies And Deal With Your Strengths And Weaknesses Biblically.* McKinney, Texas: Temperament Dynamics, LLC, 2025.

_____. *Melancholy-Sanguine Workbook: The Diplomat Pattern, How To Develop Your Natural Tendencies And Deal With Your Strengths And Weaknesses Biblically.* McKinney, Texas: Temperament Dynamics, LLC, 2025.

_____. *Melancholy-Phlegmatic Workbook: The Analyst Pattern, How To Develop Your Natural Tendencies And Deal With Your Strengths And Weaknesses Biblically.* McKinney, Texas: Temperament Dynamics, LLC, 2025.

About The Author

John T. Cocoris has devoted his life since the 1970s to develop the temperament model of behavior. John has a B.A. from Tennessee Temple University, a Masters of Theology (Th. M.) from Dallas Theological Seminary, a Masters in Counseling (M.A.) from Amberton University, and a Doctorate in Psychology (Psy.D.) from California Coast University. John was a licensed therapist in the state of Texas from 1995-2020.

John established Profile Dynamics in the early 1980s to develop and promote the temperament model of behavior for use in business and counseling. He has been a management consultant since 1984 and has worked with a variety of companies giving seminars for training managers and sales people.

John has conducted seminars in churches to help church counselors help others. John has also trained other therapists in the use of the temperament model in counseling. John has been interviewed on the radio and has been featured numerous times on COPE, a national cable TV talk show.

John and Phillip Moss formed Temperament Dynamics, LLC in 2017 to further develop, expand, and promote the temperament model of behavior.

John has written many books and manuals about the temperament model including: *Why We Do What We Do, New Insights Into The Temperament Model of Behavior; Born With A Creative Temperament, The Sanguine-Melancholy; 7 Steps To A Better You, How To Develop Your Natural Tendencies; A Parent's Manual To Helping Your Child Develop Their Natural Temperament Tendencies; A Therapist's Guide to The Temperament Model of Behavior; A Leader's Guide To Using The Temperament Model of Behavior; How To Sell Using The Temperament Model of Behavior; The* DISCII, DISC3, *DISC Strengths, and Four Temperaments Assessments, and The Temperament Profile Assessment User's Guide.*

www.ingramcontent.com/pod-product-compliance
Lightning Source LLC
Chambersburg PA
CBHW080423030426
42335CB00020B/2564

9 781948 474368